Wildlife, M

William Condry

GOMER

First impression—April 1995

ISBN 1 85902 182 4

*Printed in Wales by J. D. Lewis and Sons Ltd.,
Gomer Press, Llandysul, Dyfed.*

WILDLIFE, MY LIFE

William Condry at Craig Cerrig-gleisiad, Brecon Beacons National Park. Purple saxifrage adorns the sandstone ledges.

(Courtesy of Dafydd Davies)

CONTENTS

AUTHOR'S PREFACE

Despite its title this book can hardly claim to be an autobiography. The story of my unadventurous life would not be of the slightest interest to anybody and I have written instead about the world of nature as I have witnessed it, finding it convenient to use the passing years as a series of pegs on which to hang a succession of wildlife pictures and experiences as they are recorded in my memory or in the diaries I have kept since the days of my youth.

Certainly it is out of doors that I have always felt most at ease, well away from what Richard Jefferies called 'the endless and nameless circumstances... of house life'. What I have written here has been conceived in the open air and I pray that a fresh wind still blows through it. As time passes I become ever more convinced that it is in the wild places that we have the best hope of finding such little sanity as survives in the world.

In the preface to *Selborne* Gilbert White wrote that even if the book was not a success he would still be able to console himself that his pursuits, 'by keeping the body and mind employed, have, under Providence, contributed to much health and cheerfulness of spirits, even to old age'. I cannot wish more for my own book.

'If the warble of the first bluebird does not thrill you, know that the morning and spring of your life are past. Thus you may feel your pulse.'

'I was rich, if not in money, in sunny hours and summer days.'

Thoreau

Chapter 1

Every rock face, every leaf of grass catches the light on this golden afternoon as I reach the top of Caer Caradoc, most peak-like of the Shropshire hills. The northward view is too hazy for me to make out the spires of Shrewsbury in the valley of the Severn. In the south I see rounded heights, one behind the other, all the way to Ludlow. But it is the east-west prospects that speak to me most strongly. For these hills of Salop are a watershed in my life. Eastwards stretch the English Midlands, the land of my youth. And far in the west where the sinking sun 'bleeds along the road to Wales' (Housman is never far from my mind on this border) is where I have lived the rest of my life.

From up here on Caradoc I can see nothing of the ever expanding city where I was born. Birmingham is over thirty miles away hidden by folds in the ground. But in my mind it is clear enough as it was when I was young. My memories of south-west Birmingham, the Harborne and Edgbaston of the 1920s and 1930s, are like those of all of us who are born in outer suburbs but live to see them become inner suburbs as towns devour green pastures, perhaps leaving a few veteran oaks among the gardens to mark where hedges once divided fields or stood along lanesides.

I realise now, what I did not really appreciate as a child, that the almost rural Harborne of the 1920s was not a bad place for a young naturalist to be growing up in. There were still ploughlands out towards Tom Nocker's wood where lapwings, partridges and yellowhammers were making their last stand. In the abandoned garden of a once genteel country house a former goldfish pond was full of great crested newts, exciting creatures, far bigger and more colourful than the little brown palmate newts I am familiar with today in west Wales. On roadside tree trunks in September we sometimes found the large, spike-tailed caterpillars of the lime and poplar hawkmoths. Nothing thrilled my infant mind more than finding those wonderful caterpillars.

1

Almost on our doorstep was the Moorpool which, until our 'garden city' was built round it, had been a pool among fields. Yet despite the houses and the bowling green nearby, the quiet, tree-surrounded Moorpool still had its wild mallards and moorhens and crowds of hungry undersized perch. Harborne even had its sand martins. In a sandpit on the way to neighbouring Quinton we looked down in wonder at the little brown martins pecking out their nesting holes or swooping in with food for their young. There must be very few sand martins today so near to the centre of Birmingham as they were.

In what we called the Hillyfields (all houses now), which sloped down from the old parish church of St. Peter, there was a stream, crystal and unpolluted, where we turned the stones and found bullheads, loaches, lampreys and, best of all, crayfish. Where the stream deepened before it flowed into a willow-shaded, reedy paradise at the shallow end of Harborne Reservoir (memories of summer swimming and winter skating) there were darting shoals of minnows and occasionally some huge fish (they must have been every bit of six inches long) which an angler told us were gudgeon. In the nearby Selly Oak canal we fished for sticklebacks, which we called jack bannocks, whose breeding males, red-bellied and nearly three inches long, were our crowning delight. The Hillyfields also had a butterfly of distinction: but in those days we took the small blue for granted, not yet having learnt that this nearly black little butterfly, its wings prettily hemmed with white, was very local and special.

People have sometimes asked me where I got my preoccupation with the world of nature, but how can we ever hope to answer questions like that? All I can say is that it certainly goes back to infancy. Among my very earliest memories I see with photographic clarity two glass-topped cases in a cupboard in my bedroom. One of them is full of butterflies and moths, the other crammed with birds' eggs. They had been the treasured possession of my brother who died at the age of fourteen when I was two. He was already ill when I was born and his sick-bed comment about me, my grandmother told me in later years, was: 'I suppose he's come to take my place'. So it proved. I suppose it could be said that I have lived the life he would have lived. He, from all accounts, was a dedicated naturalist and in due course I inherited not only his boxes of specimens but also his devotion to wildlife.

Not that Dennis had made those collections himself. They had come into the family from some now forgotten relative who had evidently been a naturalist and a collector in the Victorian tradition. Those boxes of insects and birds' eggs so invaded my mind that before I knew much else about the world I could recognise red admirals, peacocks, tortoiseshells and garden tiger moths; and, though Birmingham is remote from any coast, I knew the eggs of gulls, guillemots, razorbills and oystercatchers because that case contained mostly these exciting big seabirds' eggs.

A poignant item in our family archives is a pocket diary of 1920. It was kept until June by my brother who died that year. It is full of the trivia of boyish life but one entry may be worth placing on record as a contribution to Harborne's natural history. On Saturday, June 5, Dennis wrote: 'went fishing with Uncle George at Tilt's Pool. Caught 30'. I remember Tilt. He was a dairy farmer at nearby Woodgate. Every morning he brought milk along our road in a horse and cart, ladling it into our jug from a bucket. On his farm was a pool full of little carp which were not at all easy to catch unless you were Uncle George, the Isaak Walton of our family.

I can just remember Uncle George. It was he who introduced me at a tender age to the magical world of fish; and to my juvenile eyes his life seemed to consist entirely of fishing, just as his conversation seemed all roach, dace, bleak, ruff, tench, pike and perch. He used to speak lovingly of a canal near Kings Norton and of a favourite spot along it he called 'the brimole'. Not till years later did I grasp that by this strange word he meant 'the bream-hole'.

Who can say what may influence very young minds? What about the songs our mothers sing to us? My mother was one who sang all day (so it seems to me in memory) as she went about her chores. Her repertoire was wide: popular songs, hymns or fragments of oratorios, according to her mood. But what I most enjoyed was *The Song of Hiawatha*, long passages of which she had learnt at the choral society she belonged to in her youth in Bournville. From an early age I too could sing snatches of *Hiawatha* which remain in my mind to this day. So who knows what subtle messages slid into my infant thoughts

from Longfellow's romantic evocation of wilderness America by way
of my mother's gentle contralto voice?

> Ye who love the haunts of Nature,
> Love the sunshine of the meadow,
> Love the shadow of the forest,
> Love the wind among the branches,
> And the rain-shower and the snow-storm,
> And the rushing of great rivers
> Through their palisades of pine-trees,
> And the thunder of the mountains,
> Whose innumerable echoes
> Flap like eagles in their eyries:—
> Listen to these wild traditions,
> To this Song of Hiawatha!

I suppose all of us at some time try to think back to what is our
earliest memory. Something I vividly recall is a scene of wild nature
when I was about three. We were on a family outing to the Leasowes,
a derelict estate on the way to Halesowen, that was often used by
picknickers. The Leasowes had been the very elegant property of the
eighteenth-century poet, William Shenstone, who had landscaped it
in the style of his age. But when we went there in 1921 nature had
long ago taken over. I can still feel the excitement I felt when I saw
those woods and thickets. No doubt to the adult world they were
merely a dishevelment of neglected shrubs and overgrown trees; but
for me they were a first precious encounter with wilderness. Perhaps
I expected to get a glimpse of Hiawatha himself.

There is no doubt what is my earliest memory of a wild bird. It is
a winter's day when I am still about three. Under the kitchen window
father has planted a firethorn (*Pyracantha*) to grow up the wall. This
winter it is red with fruits and today have come these unbelievably
exotic birds, the size of starlings, with crests on their heads and
scarlet and gold decorations on their wings. The local paper has
reported them in various parts of Harborne and here they now are,
gobbling our berries within two feet of me as I stand on a chair, my
face against the window. So to those who ask what made me into a
naturalist perhaps I should say that those waxwings could have had

a lot to do with it, for they must have been one of the most momentous events of my earliest years, so clearly do they remain in my mind.

In the back of my childhood memories is a paradise a couple of miles from home—the Botanical Gardens in Edgbaston. It was a great treat to be taken, once or twice a year, to what we children always called 'the Botanics'. Not that our interests were even slightly botanical. What 'the Botanics' had for us were huge gaudy parrots; monkeys with unmentionable habits; an emu with an amazing appetite for everything we offered it; and various other exotic creatures, including a terrifying bear from the Himalayas. Round the year the Botanical Gardens were the venue for various flower shows, one of which was the annual show of the National Viola Society. My father, who lived for his garden, used to enter his best violas, including a variety he had raised himself, a large, dark-blue beauty he named 'Kathleen Condry' after my sister. Then came misfortune. Because of a disease that swept through all the local viola collections, the Midlands ceased to be one of Britain's viola-growing regions; and father went in for roses and chrysanthemums instead. They became a passion that lasted for the rest of his life.

The road where I was born was called High Brow, a reflection of its elevated position not of the cultural status of its inhabitants. Until 1925, behind the houses across the road from my home, there were cornfields and hay meadows where larks sang and corncrakes rattled. But even more vividly than larks and corncrakes I remember the cuckoos. The creators of our housing estate had surrounded some of the gardens with hedges of the plum called myrobalan (*Prunus cerasifera*). It made a good, stout barrier but most summers it was stripped bare of its leaves by the black and white caterpillars of the magpie moth. At this point enter the cuckoos. For cuckoos not only have the bizarre habit of laying their eggs in other birds' nests; they also love to eat caterpillars that most other birds won't touch, those of the magpie moth for instance. So among my earliest mental pictures are these grey, long-tailed, hawk-like cuckoos that came in from the nearby fields to devour our caterpillars, cuckoos in such numbers as I have never seen since. Sometimes from our windows we could see five or six together, sprawling awkwardly on our hedge tops as they gobbled up those swarms of larvae. I have never been back to see if those plum hedges or their caterpillars are still there but I am sure the cuckoos are not. The last I heard of them was in the spring of 1951. My father, who was still living in our Harborne house, wrote to say that cuckoos had invaded the hedges after a gap of many years. This was a truly surprising influx for by then Harborne was getting finally engulfed by the urban sprawl.

Both my parents were fresh-air enthusiasts, keep-fitters. They were walkers, cyclists, swimmers, even skaters, though the only skating they ever got was on the frozen canals and pools of the occasional hard winter. Sunday was their rambling day, usually with a small group of friends and beginning each year at Easter. First there was a bus ride through what was verdant countryside to the then quiet hamlet of Bartley Green. From there we followed footpaths across the lark-loud fields towards the woods and little hills where the Stour river is born. I daresay the Stour even then was polluted by factories along its lower reaches. But up there near its springs it was a clean and merry brook gurgling amongst its pebbles under which we found little water creatures whose names we mostly did not know. But at least we could recognise water shrimps and those fascinating caddis-fly larvae that peeped from little tubes they cleverly made for themselves out of grains of sand.

On more energetic days our walks took us as far as Romsley Hill, then on to the more commanding Walton and Clent Hills. But often we were content to picnic leisurely and not get very far. Everywhere there was the world of nature to investigate however unskilfully. Not that my parents would ever have thought of themselves as naturalists; but they were interested in all we saw along the wayside and I look back on those frequent Sunday safaris as a crucial part of my education. When still very young I know I developed a warm affection for those fields, woods and modest hills we explored on our family outings, for I can remember my despair when I grew old enough to realise that sooner or later the all-devouring monster, Greater Birmingham, must inevitably one day swallow up all those green places as surely as it had already destroyed the farms and fields of earlier Harborne and Edgbaston. For years I had a recurrent nightmare of going down the lane that led from Frankley to our favourite woods along the Stour, down past the copse on the right where the turtle doves

The old Harborne Reservoir, now drained, with the clock-tower of Birmingham University in the background.

crooned in summer, on past the orchid marsh, then the wild daffodil bank, only to find that the lane now ended not in herb-rich meadows but in a vast new housing development. Since those far-off days I daresay my childhood nightmare has turned into a reality. I have no desire to go back and see.

I cannot leave my reminiscences of Harborne without mentioning one of its larger-than-life characters. Billy Turner, who lived next-door to us, was a well-known pigeon-fancier who was also devoted to wild birds and had a loathing of blood sports. He had a hugely powerful physique which was the result of rigorous training and all sorts of keep-fit activities. He was a great long-distance swimmer, slowly circling Harborne Reservoir hour after hour on a Sunday morning and clocking up a prodigious mileage. Coots, moorhens, dabchicks and wild ducks learned to accept him as some harmless water monster and he took pride in swimming close to them without causing any alarm.

He was very excited one year when a pair of the then rare great crested grebes came and nested on the reservoir. He forthwith became their self-appointed guardian and the breeding season passed successfully. Then one day in the autumn he arrived at the reservoir and met a sportsman, a gun under his arm and in his hand a pair of great crested grebes he had just shot. Billy exploded. Not waiting for any argument he picked the sportsman up and dumped him into the reservoir. Fortunately, the water just there was not deep and all the man got was a soaking; but he was never seen at the reservoir again. In due course other great crested grebes came to breed there and for all I know may have continued to do so until the reservoir was drained in later years.

Most of his life Billy kept his loft of pigeons, racing them back home from far-away places like San Sebastian. But eventually he fell out of love with pigeons and, like the poet, from the troubles of this world he turned to ducks. So when he moved house and had a bigger garden, he dug a huge pool in it and bought some mallard eggs. Soon he had a flock of ducks which he trained to fly round and come back to the pool just like pigeons to a loft. Sometimes they flew round with the neighbours' pigeons, to the astonishment of all who beheld them.

*   *   *

For me as a child our family holidays were wondrous broadeners of a young naturalist's experience. They began when I was five. Mother took my sister, me and several other children camping for the whole month of August on the then unspoilt coast of Merioneth, a brave act because she had never been camping before. (Father was to join us for his annual ten days later in the holiday.) Somehow, amid squalls of Welsh rain, mother managed to erect a very awkward, tall, square, garden tent which had a detachable roof and was completely unsuitable for camping even in the most sheltered place, which the Welsh coast certainly is not.

Throughout our first journey across Wales it had rained, the clouds had kept low and this new land had seemed a very depressing place through the windows of a slow train that pulled up every few miles at little stations with strange Welsh names: Ruabon, Acrefair, Llangollen, Bala, Llanuwchllyn, Drws-y-nant, Bont Newydd, Dolgellau, Penmaenpool and Arthog. But what a miracle to wake up next morning in our camp at Tal-y-bont, four miles north of Barmouth, to find that the storm had moved away overnight, that the·day was windstill, warm and sunny and, best of all, that only a few miles inland there was the lofty, undulating skyline of the Rhinog range with, in the foreground, a dark, round dome which, we were told, was called Moelfre. These were the first mountains we children had ever seen. The solitude was wonderful too: for that was decades before permanent caravan sites came to ruin so much of that coast.

On that first holiday our camping style could not have been more primitive. Our food was cooked on fires of sticks collected along the tide-line and all our water had to be carried in buckets from a farm-house nearly half-a-mile away. Yet though life was not always comfortable there were huge compensations. For getting to know the natural history of any wild place, nothing is so good as camping there for weeks. Soon I was well acquainted with marram grass, sea spurge, sea holly, marsh orchids, ragwort, cinnabar caterpillars, burnet moths, oystercatchers, ringed plovers, banded snails, razor shells, winkles, shore crabs and a crowd of other forms of life I had not met

Moelfre mountain, near Barmouth, a part of the Rhinog range, 'the first mountains we children had ever seen'.

with before. At the age of five I didn't know many of their names but they were my intimate friends all the same.

During our second holiday on the Merioneth coast my father and friends took me up Cader Idris. We went by train across the Mawddach estuary to Arthog and walked up from there, though I don't remember which path we followed. At the hut which then stood on the summit we were able to buy tea at what father complained was the extortionate price of sixpence a cup. (No tea at any price there today.) To get down to Dolgellau we chose that awkward track, the Foxes' Path, part of which is a long, steep, ankle-turning scree on which no sane fox would ever risk his limbs. It soon turned my ankle and I had to be carried on strong shoulders all the way down to Dolgellau. It was an ignominious end to my first mountaineering day but I had seen what a Welsh peak was like at close range—its great, grassy shoulders, its rock-strewn head, its precipices dropping to deep, black corrie lakes. It was all valuable experience for an infant mind and I have loved dear old Cader ever since.

One memory of those holidays on the shores of Cardigan Bay is very precious. Twenty-eight miles across the water we could see a humpy island lying just off the end of the long, mountainous peninsula of north Wales. It was a magic island in the sense that one day it would be there, large and clear, and then it might disappear for a week or more, the way all distant islands do. Then one morning there it would be again, standing higher than ever before, sometimes apparently floating in the air. So I made the acquaintance of Ynys Enlli (or Bardsey as the Vikings named it when they were up to no good round the Welsh coast a thousand years ago). Thirty years after I first saw it, this very alluring island was to become a part of my life.

Four successive summers we camped at Tal-y-bont and then no more. Next year, seasoned campers now and better equipped, we went to Weymouth in Dorset and saw the glories of Portland Bill and the nearby Chesil Bank with its vast terraces of sea-borne pebbles. We learnt too what treasures were to be discovered in the cliffs at Lyme Regis where my imagination was stirred for the first time by the past, not the trifling human past but the real past, the geological past. I met with Liassic fossils at just the right age for them to quicken a sense of wonder at a dimension of life we had never been taught about in school. Decades were to pass before it became normal practice to take children out of school for environmental studies.

When I got back home from Dorset I borrowed a book from Harborne Library. Called *The Earth Shown to the Children* it was full of rocks, rifts, volcanoes, earthquakes, dinosaurs, fossils; and I loved every page of it. One result was that next term at school I gave a lecture to my class-mates on the evolution of the horse, starting from a fossil called *Eohippus*, the dawn horse. Aged ten, I spoke with a self-confidence and professorial authority I have never been able to achieve on any occasion since.

In the library I found another book that entranced me: *Bevis, the story of a boy* by Richard Jefferies. Bevis was a country lad (Jefferies as a child in fact) who revelled in simple, rural pastimes that appealed to me far more than the usual boys' adventure stories. At ten years of age I felt very close to Bevis though the book had been written nearly fifty years before. Not many years later I was to soak up all that Jefferies ever wrote about nature and the countryside. Though he is not much read these days I don't doubt that his influence was huge in the early years in helping to create the wide public sympathy with nature that has been so essential to the success of the conservation movement in Britain and even in America. (Rachel Carson in *Silent Spring* acknowledges Jefferies as one of the inspirations of her life.)

In 1928 our holiday place changed from Dorset to Devon and every summer for the next nine years (sometimes at Easter too) we camped at Brixham. So we came to know and love the uncrowded south Devon of pre-war days. And we saw the last of the old Brixham trawlers, their dark-red sails disappearing into the sunset as they rounded Berry Head on the way out to their fishing grounds. There is much limestone around Brixham and wandering in the woods by our camp I became familiar with plants I had never seen before. Under the many ash trees grew wood spurge, madder, wild privet, wayfaring tree, spindle, spurge-laurel and many others. At Brixham too I first met with that impressive insect, the great green bush-cricket, an exciting find, for I had no idea such a splendid creature existed. And a fine colourful moth I used to find there (which I have never seen since) was the Jersey tiger. It was not uncommon and showed itself quite conspicuously by day along the hedgebanks in August.

It was in Devon that I first saw the courtship display of buzzards. One Easter holiday I was in the woods along the tidal Dart just upriver from Kingswear. High in the upper breezes a pair of buzzards were circling and wailing with excitement. Then one after the other they came plunging almost vertically for hundreds of feet, did a sharp U-turn just above the trees to go arrowing back up to where they had started from. This manoeuvre, astonishing to my young eyes, they repeated over and over until, tiring of the play, they floated quietly away. I have been charmed by buzzards ever since.

Two circumstances in my mid-teens I have reason to be grateful for. First, that I was given a bicycle and so acquired a magic freedom to go off and explore a wider world; and second, that my teens were in the 1930s when there was so much less traffic on the roads than there is today. How even more idyllic (except that the roads were much rougher) cycling must have been for the previous generation when there was nothing more dangerous than horse-drawn vehicles to contend with! My father, when a youth, had one of those awkward contraptions, a penny-farthing, which had to be mounted from the top of a wall. He used to tell us what a revolution it was when the modern bike, complete with pneumatic tyres (they called it the safety bicycle), became popular in the 1890s. People then took to the open road as never before. I like to think of my father and his Clarion Cycling Club friends peddling their way from Birmingham to far-away places like Betws-y-coed or Aberystwyth, journeys that could otherwise be made in one day only by train.

Forty years later I in my turn was off on my bike on many a Saturday or Sunday jaunt, sometimes alone but usually with my closest friend and fellow birdwatcher, Harold Wright. I was not then one of nature's early risers but Harold was, and he would get me out of bed, without stirring the rest of the house, by flinging gravel at my bedroom window soon after dawn. Often we made first for the Clent Hills which gave us a view westwards across a great reach of unknown country away to the far blue horizons of the mountains of Wales. Another joy of the Clent Hills in those days was that even in winter we could sometimes hear woodlarks singing up there. To me that music was and still is the loveliest of all bird songs, so pure, so varied, so controlled.

From the Clent Hills Harold and I went free-wheeling down the western lanes into lowland Worcestershire. In spring skylarks sang over fields of short, green corn, lapwings yodelled above their nests and greenfinches laughed along the hedgerows as we sped in the early morning silence through villages still asleep. Sometimes, getting over the Severn at Bewdley, we went right across that part of Worcestershire into a region that became very special to us because there, in south Shropshire and north Herefordshire, the land began to get stronger, the lanes climbed to wilder places and we felt we were getting close to country very different from the Midlands.

One of the delights of reaching so far west was that somewhere about Ludlow we began to hear the trilling and piping of wood warblers in all the steep hillside oakwoods, a song of which we knew nothing further east. That region also charmed us with its little rivers that came winding down from the hills, especially the Teme and the Lugg which were born across the border in Wales. Along them we saw more dippers, grey wagtails and sandpipers than we had ever seen before. One day, early in May, we found a new wildflower, a creamy-pink, somewhat orchid-like spike quite without leaves, growing at a streamside in deep shade under hazel bushes. We had no idea what this strange, gloom-loving plant could be until back home, looking it up in the books, we found it was toothwort, a parasite on the roots of hazel and various trees.

As I flick through my diaries of the thirties there are scenes which come back as bright as colour-slides projected onto a screen. There was the day in May when Harold and I wandered into a bluebell wood near Chaddesley Corbett. Suddenly, from just in front of us, a female blackbird rose from the ground and flew away with yells of alarm. There, right at our feet, was her nest with five blue-green eggs surrounded by bluebells all in flower. Never since have I seen a blackbird's nest on the ground: on the side of an earth bank, yes, but not on the level floor of a wood. That nest among the bluebells would have made a wonderful colour photograph; but in those days, though colour film was beginning to be available, we thought only in terms of black and white. (Nearly sixty years later Harold Wright remains a black-and-white photographer of great merit.)

My youthful diaries chronicle many a frolic in search of little owls. Introduced from the Continent these mini-owls had invaded the Midlands with enthusiasm and had become very familiar to us as they perched boldly in broad daylight on walls and poles, defying us with glaring, yellow eyes. As we cycled home along the lanes at dusk we loved to hear them greeting or challenging each other across the fields with musical cries. Clipped into my diary of 1936 there is a circular from the British Trust for Ornithology (then only four years old) announcing that Miss Alice Hibbert-Ware was studying the diet of little owls and that she needed to examine pellets of their undigested food remains found in nests or under perches. It was just the sort of inquiry to appeal to energetic youngsters with a passion for climbing trees. So for a couple of years Harold and I looked into every hollow tree we could find, collecting these pellets full of shiny-black beetles' wing-cases. Eventually Miss Hibbert-Ware was able to prove conclusively that, contrary to the then accepted belief, the little owl was primarily an eater of beetles and other invertebrates, and that it was certainly not a mass-killer of pheasant chicks as had long been claimed by most gamekeepers.

Gamekeepers! How we loathed the keepers of those days when, creeping quietly through the coverts, we came upon the rotting bodies of the so-called vermin which gamekeepers nailed in rows along the rails to prove to their employers that the pheasants were being efficiently protected from predators. These gibbets usually included stoats, weasels, crows, jays and magpies along with, and this really sickened us, our beloved little owls, tawny owls, sparrowhawks and kestrels.

Happily, gamekeeping had come to an end in the woods we most frequented along the upper Stour, and Harold and I were lucky enough to get permission from Lord Cobham of Hagley Hall to go birdwatching in one of his former preserves called Ell Wood and to put up hides: for photography was now our passion. In those days bird-at-nest pictures were all the fashion and with a heavy, awkward, plate camera Harold photographed various small woodland birds feeding their young. Then when we got more ambitious we built elaborate hides in tree-tops and were able to observe and photograph sparrowhawks.

14

Chiffchaff's nest, Ell Wood, Worcestershire, 1938.

Harold Wright

Whitethroat's nest, Ell Wood, Worcestershire, 1938.

Harold Wright

Female sparrowhawk, Ell Wood, Worcestershire, July 1939.

Harold Wright

My diary records precious moments such as the first time we watched a female sparrowhawk's careful approach and heard her subdued, quavering calls from nearby perches. At last she came to the nest and from a breath-taking ten-feet range we saw her tear her prey into morsels which she fed very gently to her newly hatched young. One photograph we longed for but never got was of a male sparrowhawk. At all the nests we photographed, the young were fed entirely by the female. If ever a male did come he simply dropped food into the nest but never stayed. We got an exciting glimpse of a slate-blue back and a pink breast and he was gone.

Preoccupied with birds we had little time for any other creatures except that we were always conscious of squirrels, for they shared the tree-tops with us and the birds. Unobtrusively the American greys were spreading across the Worcestershire countryside. But the red squirrels had not yet said goodbye and we took both of them for granted, not suspecting the tragedy that was taking place—that the greys would soon be everywhere and the reds would be only a memory. It is curious that even now, six decades later, no one can say for certain why the red squirrels have vanished from so many of their ancient homelands.

*   *   *

My education was not without its problems around that time. Early in my youth my parents had been advised that a budding naturalist like me should be taking biology, a subject that was then beginning to spread through the schools. But George Dixon School in City Road, Edgbaston, which I entered aged eleven, though it was science orientated, did not yet teach biology; and in the sixth form it offered only maths, physics and chemistry, for none of which I had much aptitude, being more interested in languages and literature. Then just as I was about to enter the sixth form, apparently doomed to become an unwilling scientist, the scenario changed. Sam Brown, the headmaster, a man of science, retired and, blessed event, in his place came Howard C. Cooksey, an arts man, one of whose first acts was to set up an arts sixth form, something new in the school's history. So was created an untrodden world which I cheerfully entered, a step I have never regretted. I was able to carry on with Latin, French, English and history, and have loved them all ever since. This does not mean that I have no regrets about never having another lesson in science after the age of sixteen. Many a time down the years I have wished I had a better grasp of the basics of chemistry, physics, zoology, botany and geology. I blame the system that forced us to make such an early and irrevocable choice between the arts and the sciences. Far better to have let them flow on together right through schooldays and beyond.

From school my next move was to Birmingham University in 1936 when the arts faculty was still located in the city centre at the old Mason College building in Edmund Street. I looked round for a college natural history society or a birdwatching club but there was none. In fact, a whole year went by before I discovered a fellow bird enthusiast. Ray Perry was a student of English and little dreamt at that period of his life that he was destined to become the well-known expert on woodland ecology that he is today. He came from Staffordshire and soon he was taking me round his favourite birding haunts near Enville. Here was a type of country quite new to me—an expanse of dry, sandy heath with magnificent Scots pines widely spread. There Ray showed me birds I had only read about in books: woodcock, nightjar and hawfinch. We also looked for red-backed shrikes which Ray could remember there a few seasons before. But by then they had gone from the whole of the Midlands and would soon be rare all over Britain. It was with Ray Perry that I first got into the heart of the Wyre Forest which, in the 1930s, was still a place of immeasurable solitude. One day we picked some edible boleti. It was lunch-time and all we needed was a frying pan. We had not gone very far when, to my amazement, Ray reached a long arm into a hollow tree and produced a frying pan! Did he, I wondered, have frying pans cached in strategic hollow trees all over the district?

There was a day when Ray and I did not do very well. We had read about that rare bird, the marsh warbler, a colony of which was reported to breed every year in an osier bed along the Avon in south Worcestershire. So we got up at four o'clock one summer morning and cycled the thirty-five miles to the banks of the Avon, eagerly anticipating the sight of our first marsh warbler. It was not to be. Certainly in that horsefly-infested jungle of little willows along the quiet river there were more birds singing than we had ever heard concentrated into so small an area. And I don't doubt that while most were just reed warblers and sedge warblers, a few of them must have been marsh warblers. But we were never sure which was which. Let our excuse be that, as well as having binoculars that were little better than opera-glasses, we did not really know what we should be looking for. The field guides of today were still undreamed of and not even *The Handbook of British Birds* had yet appeared. Better than any book would have been someone to help us in the field. But in those days birdwatchers were nearly as scarce as marsh warblers.

One who could have sorted things out for us was Anthony Harthan who lived near the Avon, was the author of *The Birds of Worcestershire* and was a marsh warbler expert. But I didn't get to know Anthony until long after I had left the Midlands for Wales and he was on holiday near Harlech. Then he told me how marsh warblers, when at their peak of population, nested not only among riverside osiers but also in the nearby bean-fields, an astonishingly dry habitat. These days the marsh warbler is scarcer than ever. So if I am ever going to have a good chance of seeing one, I shall need to go to the Continent or have a winter holiday in Zambia where my friend Robert Stjernstedt tells me he has helped to catch plenty of migrant marsh warblers in mist nets in order to ring them.

Let me end these memories of the Midlands with a majestic chorus of starlings. It is dusk on a winter's afternoon, lectures are over for the day and we troop out of Birmingham University into Chamberlain Square. And there, high above the noise of the traffic, we hear the shrill, massed choir of tens of thousands of excited starlings which come from the countryside to roost every night on the city-centre buildings. It is an amazing manifestation of bird life and bird vitality. Today I'm told it no longer happens and if this is so the heart of the city must be a much duller place on winter evenings.

Chapter 2

What a debt we youngsters of the thirties owed to the Youth Hostels Association (founded 1930)! Without those cheap and simple hostels we could never have got round the countryside so easily by foot and by cycle. We stayed at many a hostel from Shrewsbury to the coast of Cardigan Bay but our favourite was always one near Llanidloes at the hamlet of Y Fan which in those days was known universally as 'Van', a place famous in the annals as the site of one of the richest lead-mines in Wales.

Here in the late 1930s, years after the mine had closed, the youth hostel occupied what had been the mine-manager's house. What made it so dear to us hostellers was the warden, Elizabeth Jones, a golden-hearted Welsh lady famous far and wide for the way she mothered us all (in sharp contrast with one or two other female wardens elsewhere who were notorious termagants). Elizabeth Jones, a native of Aber-soch near Pwllheli, had come to Van because her late husband, a miner, had found work there. She clearly loved being a warden and if she broke the hostel rules, as she did most of the time, she could always plead she did not understand them because her grasp of English was not very strong. So she ignored the rules, we ignored the rules and everyone was happy, except the officials who occasionally turned up on tours of inspection and who sometimes expressed their horror at the lax way the place was run. But what could they do? Even they could see that nothing would ever change Mrs Jones who couldn't read or remember the regulations, yet was an outstandingly successful warden.

Exploring the Plynlimon (Pumlumon) country from Van hostel (I was usually with Harold Wright or Ray Perry) we soon got to know the many old lead-mines whose ruins year after year were nesting places for kestrels, barn owls, stock doves, redstarts and pied and grey wagtails. Once we found a huge, completely inaccessible raven's nest balanced improbably on top of a high wall. Then as time went on we felt curious about the whole long saga of lead-mining. In the villages

21

we inquired round for ex-miners but found they had mostly gone underground for ever, long before their time, as we could see from the dates on many a gravestone. The lead-mining communities, we learned, had been decimated by tuberculosis and their descendants were still not free of it.

Today some of the lead-mines survive as crumbling walls and grey vomits of poisoned earth. But the Van mine, when I knew it in the late 1930s, though its underground workings were all flooded, was virtually intact above ground, its buildings in fair condition. The whole site, where a thousand men had once worked, was wrapped in a ghost-town atmosphere and one day I had a truly moving experience: I remember getting a key off somebody and going into what had been the mine-manager's office and finding, still on his desk, a ledger recording the last consignment of lead ever to leave Van mine in, I think, about 1921. For eighteen years or so that ledger had lain ready on the desk as if the mine had simply closed for a holiday instead of for ever. And there was I reading that final entry and feeling I ought to draw a line across the page and write: 'Here ended the famous Van mine which brought much wealth to a few and great misery to many'.

Van lead-mine near Llanidloes. A postcard of the 1920s showing the mine
a few years after it had closed.

22

Sheltering Van youth hostel from the westerly gales there was at that time a long row of tall old Corsican pines which gave a distinctive personality to the house. Through their branches the wind sighed or roared, a lovely sound to listen to from the open windows of the dormitories at night. Tawny owls often perched in them, hooting and shrieking; and now and then there was a rarer voice, the moaning cry of a long-eared owl which was sometimes answered by others farther up the valley. This rare owl we longed to see as well as hear and in its pursuit we went on long walks towards the moorlands of Plynlimon by way of the Clywedog valley which was not yet drowned by the reservoir of today. It was on the whole a treeless district and we guessed that the long-eared owls must be living in the widely scattered squares or lines of conifers planted as windbreaks to shelter the sheep on draughty hillsides. Eventually, after a huge amount of foot-slogging, we learned to spot these owls high up in the trees, their bodies pressed against the trunk and drawn up grotesquely tall and thin to make them seem like a swelling on the bark. We also saw them fly from nests which were not of their making but were the old tenements of carrion crows.

From Van the next youth hostel westwards was thirteen crow-flight miles away at Ponterwyd and we got into the habit of walking there over the top of Plynlimon which for several years became our favourite mountain. We enjoyed reaching the summit cairns where the Bronze Age had buried its notables. From up there we saw that huge panorama south to the Beacons, north to Snowdon, east to where we told ourselves we could make out the Clent Hills, and west across the sea to Bardsey Island. We paid our respects to the sources of the rivers of which Plynlimon is the famous mother—Wye, Severn and Rheidol. We splashed across the marshes and climbed the cliffs, getting to know more and more about ravens, peregrines, wheatears, skylarks, golden plovers and ring ouzels. We swore, though not too seriously, that one day we would write a ten-volume monograph about meadow pipits. For of all the upland birds it was these lively little pipits that we came upon everywhere we went, their tinkling songs falling from the sky to emphasise the quietness of the empty hills. (No low-flying military jets in those happy times.)

Plynlimon near the source of the Wye.

In the high peatbogs we searched for flint arrowheads dropped by Bronze Age hunters, for many have been found up there. But all we ever picked up was a modern penny which we pushed down into the peat in the hope that someone would find it a thousand years hence. Sometimes we went down into the moorland valleys where we found lonely shepherds' houses (all had long been abandoned to the barn owls) and many pathetic cottage remains which spoke of days when a scattered community, forced into the uplands by poverty, had struggled for existence in a world of hostile climate and unkind soils.

These old Plynlimon houses, some semi-abandoned, some totally deserted, some already ruinating, became a part of our lives: Blaen Hafren, Hore, Hengwm Annedd, Lluest Newydd, Nant-y-llyn, Maes-nant, Drosgol, Llechwedd Mawr, Lluest-y-rhos, Hyddgen. The few that were still roofed we used occasionally for shelter. Once at semi-ruined Hore I climbed part-way into the space between the bedroom ceiling and the roof and found it full of grown-up young barn owls and their two parents. Seeing my head and shoulders suddenly appear they fluttered about the loft like great white moths until they escaped by scuttling over my bowed head. It was a strange experience to have a whole flock of owls running over my head and down my back to freedom.

In terms of human esteem Plynlimon has had a chequered career. Several centuries ago it was widely believed to be the highest mountain in Wales (in fact there are about forty that are higher); and the painfully crude Gough map of c. 1350 shows rivers radiating from the vicinity of Plynlimon to most parts of Wales. But as people, especially the mining speculators, got to know the mountains better, Plynlimon steadily diminished in popular esteem and by the eighteenth century it was getting a really bad press as a dreary moorland very dangerous for its bogs and certainly not worth climbing. Happily by the time George Borrow climbed it in 1854 Plynlimon was back in favour. He loved the whole place, its views, its river sources, its russet autumnal beauty. With him he had a local shepherd who, to Borrow's delight, still held on to the belief that Plynlimon was a mountain of phenomenal size. I would like to have been there to hear that shepherd solemnly declare: 'I question whether there is a higher hill in the world'.

Barn owls nested in many of the deserted shepherds' houses on the Plynlimon moorlands.

Nant-y-moch house and chapel, looking towards Plynlimon. The site is now covered by a hydro-electric reservoir.

One April evening I went off alone to Plynlimon with my bicycle and my sleeping bag. I followed the rough winding track up the Rheidol river from Ponterwyd to Nant-y-moch which was then the highest inhabited farm in the valley and lived in by two bachelor brothers named James who were reputed to have sold their skulls to a museum (to be collected at a later date!) because these skulls were thought by anthropologists to have a peculiarly primitive shape dating back to the very earliest people known to have lived on those uplands. My visit took place long years before Nant-y-moch house was demolished to make way for the present reservoir and before the very rough track had been turned into the tourist road of today.

I rode or carried my bike as high up the mountain as I could and then went on without it. In those days the most exciting bird in my life was the peregrine and my aim was to sleep as close to a pair of peregrines as I could (without disturbing them) for the pleasure of sharing the dawn with them. It was nearly dark when I reached their crag and there was no sign of them as I unrolled my sleeping bag on a wide ledge about thirty feet directly under the nest.

The next day came in calm, cold and cloudless and I watched the cliffs slowly take shape above me. There was complete quietness except for the distant murmur of water amongst rocks. Then from higher up the corrie the piping notes of a ring ouzel came faintly out of the near darkness. It was still dimmit-light when the peregrines awoke; and for the next ten minutes I listened to their dawn duet. This was a softly uttered, tremulous series of beautiful notes which conveyed a feeling of suppressed excitement. Or maybe I was the one who was excited, for it was a wonderful sound to hear in that wild place. Then I suppose one of the peregrines must have gone off hunting, for there was silence again except for the ring ouzel still bringing in the dawn; and the spluttering notes of a wheatear just below me. As I made my way down to collect my bicycle I heard no more of the peregrines. But it had been a dawn to remember more vividly than perhaps any dawn before or since.

Hengwm Annedd, a long-abandoned house on the Cardiganshire uplands under Plynlimon.

Another Plynlimon memory is of a wild autumn night when darkness had overtaken me miles up into the moors. Sheets of heavy rain were sweeping across and volleys of thunder were echoing round the hills. I had had a punishing day and crept exhausted into the long-abandoned but still roofed house at Hengwm Annedd. By a mercy I found on the hearth enough dry jackdaw-provided sticks to make a fire and I sat a long time in front of it, happily making toast and wondering about those who had lived or tried to live in that lonely place. Then I slept till daybreak.

I can't leave those pre-war Plynlimon days without a thought about the Clywedog Reservoir that lies along the mountain road between Machynlleth and Llanidloes. Overlooking the reservoir there is a spacious car-park, picnic site and viewpoint above the narrow, winding lake. Yet though spectacular it is not a scene I can admire because as I look down on that deep reservoir I see only the valley it destroyed—a tranquil, totally unspoilt, almost unknown gorge with the lovely Clywedog stream hastening over its rocks and vanishing down through woodlands on its way to join the Severn.

It is not merely this reservoir that I dislike. I see no real beauty in any man-drowned valleys however essential they are to industrial-isation and to cities far away. I heartily detest Brianne in Carmarthen-shire, especially as it has a loathsomeness of conifers around it. For the same reason I never rejoice at Vyrnwy (Llyn Efyrnwy). Nor have I ever loved those waters under which the City of Birmingham drowned the beautiful Elan valley. And I understand something of the feelings of those Welsh patriots who still feel so bitter about the City of Liverpool's reservoir in the Tryweryn valley near Bala where a small Welsh community was evicted. If we could get access to all the schemes that lie in planners' desks, how many other valleys would we find earmarked as possible reservoir sites?

★   ★   ★

The years were passing but still the family went on with our annual summer camping. Just why, after so many Augusts in Devon, we decided to go elsewhere is something I have forgotten. The year was 1938, the clouds of war were not far over the horizon and soon those family holidays would be over for ever; and so would my lark-happy youth. We camped at Manorbier on the Pembrokeshire coast, on a patch of greensward half-way between the shore and those medieval castle walls that have long watched the sea from their green hill. For five weeks we explored that wild coast all the way from Tenby to where the breakers unceasingly pound the shore at Freshwater West.

We walked out to the great headlands of Stackpole and St Govan's. We bathed unnoticed at Barafundle though that delightful beach was then the strictly private domain of nearby Stackpole Court. We saw Bosherston's ponds white all over with lilies. We looked in wonder at the Stack Rocks, twin pillars of limestone standing lonely in the sea and thronged with uncountable seabirds. And we met with a new bird altogether, that graceful, red-billed, red-legged crow, the chough, which so clearly enjoyed being flung about the sky by all the winds of Heaven.

Splendid caterpillars crawl in and out of memory when I think of those Manorbier days. At the laneside up past the castle grew a fine bush of wild privet and peering into it one day my mother spotted two full-grown larvae of the privet hawkmoth. In the whole world of British insects there are few creatures more spectacular then these large, plump, apple-green caterpillars decorated with purple bars across their flanks and ending with a curved blue spike. They were a special excitement to me because although at home in winter I had occasionally dug up privet hawkmoth pupae from under Harborne's privet hedges, the caterpillars of summer had always eluded me.

There were other delights at Manorbier. That was a summer when those busy daylight visitors from south Europe, the hummingbird hawkmoths, were arriving on the south Wales coast in exceptional numbers. All around our camp grew their food plant, the fragrant, yellow-flowered lady's bedstraw, and I watched the moths laying eggs on its leaves. When I looked closer I found well-grown caterpillars too, showing that the migrant moths had been coming in for several weeks. There was, however, a melancholy side to this story. When I looked them up in a moth book I found that hummingbird hawkmoths, though they pupate successfully, cannot survive the British winter and that all their egg-laying was futile.

Next year (August 1939) we camped at Croyde near Barnstaple on the north coast of Devon. It was a dispirited few weeks as we tried in vain to convince ourselves that war was not imminent. So passed what was to be our last family holiday because, long before peace returned, mother had died. Like my father she was a life-long pacifist; but while his pacifism came from people like Keir Hardie and the Independent Labour Party, she was a Quaker-style pacifist, having been an attender of Friends' Meetings at Bournville in her younger days.

For me that north Devon holiday was partly redeemed by finding myself in well-known territory. This was 'the country of the two rivers' (Taw and Torridge) with which I was thoroughly familiar through reading *Tarka the Otter* and other stories by Henry Williamson to whose writings I was then devoted. The Richard Jefferies of his generation, Williamson was second only to Jefferies in helping to create that popular sympathy for wildlife which after the war was to lead to the nature conservation movement that is still growing in strength.

Other memories of Croyde are of walking out to the end of Baggy Point, a windswept, wave-lashed, raven-croaking headland; and of wandering among the plant-rich dunes of Braunton Burrows. It was at Croyde that I first saw a cirl bunting. It was singing on the telegraph wires, its notes louder, quicker and more clearly pronounced than those of the nearby yellowhammers. In later years, I'm told, the cirl bunting disappeared from north Devon and has not yet returned. I haven't either.

Chapter 3

After war came in 1939 my nature diaries find less and less to record. They fade out completely in 1940 and do not return to life until the end of the war is in sight. Not that this gap was in any way a loss. I have no wish to be reminded of those desolate years when madness ruled the globe even more than usual, when bombs rained down on Birmingham and when my mind got switched off for months at a stretch from any thought of the natural world and other forms of sanity. I was sad when Harold Wright, who did not share the pacifism on which I had been nurtured, went off to the war; but he survived it and I treasure a comment he made about his spell of active service in France before the evacuation at Dunkirk: 'Did I ever tell you that my father was mentioned in despatches in the '14-'18 war? I wonder what they said? I would like to think it was something like: *Studied reed warblers in a wet ditch under Stuka bombing,* as happened to me in 1940'.

A memory of *A Shropshire Lad.* The River Corve was one of A. E. Housman's 'streams too broad for leaping'.

One of my happier wartime memories is linked back to my school-days when as a prize I was given a copy of Housman's *A Shropshire Lad*. I took to Housman immediately and soon I could, and still can, recite from memory many of his lines, especially those referring to places Harold and I had cycled to: Knighton, Shrewsbury, Uricon, Wenlock, Wrekin, Bredon, Ludlow, Clee, Buildwas and Wyre; and those 'streams too broad for leaping': Severn, Teme, Clun, Onny and Corve. Years later, when war was raging, there came a day like a shaft of sunlight in a stormy sky. On a perfect spring morning I took that delightful train that used to chug slowly from the Severn at Bewdley up between 'the wild green hills of Wyre' to Cleobury Mortimer where it came clear of the forest to run through a land of cherry orchards which that day were all in perfection of white blossom. Everyone knows Housman's cherries: 'Loveliest of trees the cherry now is hung with bloom along the bough'; and on that train journey over and down to Tenbury Wells and Woofferton *A Shropshire Lad* came poignantly back into my mind, especially when I saw woodlands being clear-felled for the purposes of war and I found myself reciting:

> Give me a land of boughs in leaf
> A land of trees that stand;
> Where trees are fallen there is grief;
> I love no leafless land.

1946 was the year I first fell under the spell of the mountains of Eryri, known to non-Welsh speakers as Snowdonia. It was also the year I was married. For some time Penny had wanted to become a youth hostel warden and this she achieved in 1946. Her hostel was a beautiful old house named Cae Dafydd which stands in that exquisite Snowdonian valley called Nanmor. We were married on a day of perfect April sunlight and on the way back from our wedding in Llŷn, the driver of our hired car, evidently a local patriot, decided we ought to see some of the sights. Among these was Lloyd-George's grave which is near Cricieth in the mausoleum designed by Sir Clough Williams-Ellis. I remember being totally unmoved by this edifice, having then no more admiration of politicians than I have now. But the site was altogether beautiful—the bank of a river for which, over the years since then, I have developed a special affection.

Mountains of Eryri—Lliwedd, Snowdon, Crib Goch and Crib-y-ddysgl from Llynnoedd Mymbyr.

It is the Dwyfor which flows down from Cwm Pennant, a valley whose name is known to all who speak Welsh because of an evocative poem written in its praise. Its much quoted last lines are:

> Pam, Arglwydd, y gwnaethost Gwm Pennant mor dlws,
> A bywyd hen fugail mor fyr?
> (Why, Lord, did you make Cwm Pennant so beautiful
> And the life of an old shepherd so brief?)

I have often been back to Cwm Pennant to walk its horseshoe of hills and to seek plants on their craggy summits. The highest of these is a shapely dome called Moel Hebog which on clear days filled our western view from the youth hostel. To the east of us towered another popular mountain, Cnicht, but this was hidden from us by the forbidding rocks of Yr Arddu. All the Snowdonian summits, except (these days) Snowdon itself, are fragments of true wilderness, but there is a special harshness and barrenness about Yr Arddu where naked rock climbs to naked rock all the way to the top of the ridge.

34

Up there on the bare crags of Yr Arddu, though in height it is nothing of a mountain, I first realised that although the Plynlimon uplands are such superb walking country, there is something extra-special about those much craggier mountains further north.

Six months after we were married Penny and I went off on a better-late-than-never honeymoon. The hostel closed for the winter in October and now here we were camping in south Pembrokeshire on the very spot below Manorbier castle where I had camped with my parents just before the war. So Penny and I walked the autumnal cliffs, enjoying the sun, the wind, the rain and the heaving seas; we saw choughs and ravens playing in the upper air; said farewell to the year's last wheatears; and at night we listened to the wails and groans of water rails in a nearby marsh.

We also took it into our heads to go and make the acquaintance of Ronald Lockley whose books about living close to nature were then becoming well known. There is nothing like a war for shaking society up and filling people with an urge to start afresh with new ideas of living. So Lockley's writings about throwing everything up and going to be a farmer, however struggling, on an uninhabited Pembrokeshire island, came just at the right moment to have a great romantic appeal to many readers, especially the young. The coming of war had ended Lockley's brave experiment on Skokholm and by 1946 he had acquired Island Farm which, despite its name, is not a farm on an island but on a great, cliffy, north Pembrokeshire headland with the sea on three sides.

Seeking out Ronald Lockley was for us a momentous occasion, but, as so often happens, we did not recognise it as such till long afterwards. We had wanted to meet him because he was one of the few at that time who was doing anything about nature conservation in Wales. We were keen to learn more about the West Wales Field Society which he had recently helped to create, mainly to protect seabirds, choughs, ravens and peregrines from egg-collectors; and seals from persecution by fishermen and trigger-happy shooters.

By various changes of bus we made our way from Manorbier in the south of Pembrokeshire to Dinas Cross in the north. From there we walked up the tilted, breezy fields of Island Farm till we found Ronald Lockley in the middle of threshing his corn. Leaving his helpers to get on with it for a while he told us all about the new field society and how it had originated as the Pembrokeshire Bird-protection Society, founded in 1938, and how it now hoped to extend its influence into the neighbouring counties of Carmarthen and Cardigan. It was anxious to win wide public support for its aims, chief among which was the creation of nature reserves. Today, after half a century, such a programme seems routine enough. But immediately after the Second World War such ideas had the excitement of novelty and bold thinking. So many things we now take for granted—wildlife trusts, official nature conservation, nature trails, reserves, national parks, outdoor pursuit centres, environmental studies, Forestry Commission and other visitor centres—all these were still in the future.

*   *   *

After a season of hostel wardening Penny and I decided we had other lives to live and in mid-January we moved forty miles south to a primitive cottage called Bwlch Gwair which stood at a thousand feet on the south-western approaches to Plynlimon above Ponterwyd.

Bwlch Gwair, Ponterwyd, our first cottage. It was almost buried in the snow-drifts of early 1947.

And there a week later we got the full force of the century's most ferocious Welsh blizzards. For nearly the first three weeks of 1947 the weather had been quite soft. Then without warning, about January 19, a north-east gale, full of snow, began to rage down the mountain slopes and the uplands were soon deeply buried. The wind grew ever colder and day after day the air was white with fine-grained snow that raced past our windows and piled itself to unbelievable depths. Even the shepherds, usually so weather-conscious, were caught napping, their flocks still up on the moors. Few of those sheep could be reached through the blizzards and they died in hundreds, especially those which had sought the shelter of hollows and got buried under drifts many yards deep. Not even the oldest inhabitants could remember such weather. Occasionally there were days when the cold seemed to be easing, the wind edging round to the west. But these were futile hopes. Time after time the mild Atlantic fronts just failed to get in and instead the blizzards came back. At least we did not suffer from power-cuts; for in that little cottage there was no power to cut. At last, during a brief lull in the storm, we made our escape from the uplands, leaving our cottage completely buried under a mountainous drift from which we crawled out as from an igloo. The main road had been opened and once we had struggled down to the village a bus got us to the coast at Aberystwyth.

It happened that a few weeks before the bad weather started we had heard from Ronald Lockley that the newly formed Field Studies Council was planning to open a study centre at Dale Fort on the shores of Milford Haven, that the interior of the building, which then belonged to the West Wales Field Society, was in a bad state of neglect and that willing hands were needed to spruce it up and make it ready for occupation. Though we had been warned it would be like cleaning out the Augean Stables, Penny and I had volunteered; and now that we had managed to get to Aberystwyth we took the opportunity to move on down the coast to Dale, hoping for milder weather in that normally frost-free corner of Wales.

But that winter not even Dale escaped. Instead of being a haven for storm-driven birds, south-west Pembrokeshire in February, 1947, became a death-trap for thousands. The day after we reached there the weather turned arctic yet again. Everywhere we went, when we dared to venture into the lanes or along the cliff slopes, we found the dead and the dying: starlings, redwings and blackbirds in hundreds along with snipe, jack snipe, woodcock, curlews, lapwings and water rails. We wondered how many had taken off from the cliffs in desperation and perished at sea.

As a final memory of those Dale blizzards, let me tell of my encounter with a meadow pipit, a bird that normally lives on insects and other small creatures. But what hope was there for insectivores in weather like that? On a day of near hurricane, when I had to crawl to get to the end of Dale Point and could see only a few yards because of drifting snow, this pipit came to take shelter in the lee of my crouching body; and there it ate blades of shrivelled, brown grass, nibbling them off fragment by fragment. If I forget everything else about that awesome weather at Dale I think I will remember that little bird's determination to survive.

By the middle of March migrant wheatears were telling me it was spring and in my mind's ear I could hear the larks beginning to sing over Plynlimon. But Penny was committed to staying on awhile in Pembrokeshire. The bird observatory on Skokholm Island, closed during the war, had been re-opened the previous year by John Fursdon and was now to be under the wardenship of Peter Conder. So after I left Dale, Penny, having volunteered her services as cook, went to live for a spell among the puffins, shearwaters, petrels and spring migrants for which Skokholm is famous. She still remembers the magic of the early mornings when she woke in her little tent on the cliffs above South Haven close to the white figure head of the *Alice Williams,* the wooden schooner which was wrecked on Skokholm with its cargo of coal soon after Ronald Lockley settled there in 1927. Several times while on Skokholm Penny was lucky enough to accompany parties who landed on Grassholm which is seven miles out to sea beyond Skokholm and is home for thousands of gannets.

Among the observatory visitors Penny cooked for on Skokholm was Ludwig Koch who was to become so famous on the radio both for his pioneer recordings of bird voices and for his brave but excruciating attempts to speak English. There was also Sir Julian Huxley, at that time director-general of Unesco. No doubt during his stay this great man treated the company to many words of wisdom but after half a century all that Penny can remember is that over supper one evening he explained how every night before going to sleep, he carefully rehearsed everything he had planned for the morrow, the idea being that his subconscious mind would then work all night on this agenda and so produce more efficient results next day. Penny has tried to do this ever since but with mixed results!

When I returned north to mid-Wales I found that our igloo was a cottage again and that most of the snow had gone off the lower hills, though the deepest drifts, impacted into ice, were to streak the landscape for many weeks to come. This was the only spring I have ever seen wheatears perched singing on crests of snow. But how beautiful they were in that brilliant reflected sunlight! That spring and summer had an ugly side too—the stench of rotting carrion where huddles of sheep had died in hollows or in the lee of walls where snow had buried them. It was a reek that was to hang on the moorland air right through till autumn.

Despite nauseating odours and a severe shortage of some birds because of winter losses, 1947 was a good summer. Penny came and went several times to and from stints of cooking for Skokholm observatory and when she was finally home in our little hill cottage she got busy with her loom and wove scarves and head-squares for all her family and friends, for she had not yet become absorbed in gardening as she was to be a few years later. In fact there was no garden or fence at Bwlch Gwair. Sheep grazed right to the doorstep. Only a few yards away snipe drummed and called all through spring and curlews yodelled over their nests.

That spring I passed my time (Harold Wright joining me whenever he could) mainly in observing and mapping the local birdlife, especially that of the secluded Myherin valley to which I walked almost daily over the hills. This treeless moorland valley with a high waterfall at its head had recently been planted with spruces by the Forestry Commission, and what greatly interested us was to see how the little trees were attracting woodland and bush birds to an area of grassland that probably had not seen a woodland bird for centuries. The response of the wildflowers was also a delight, especially the heather which began to spread across the slopes as soon as the sheep

Cock whinchat at Bwlch Gwair, Ponterwyd, spring 1947.

Harold Wright

A lesser redpoll nesting in the young plantations of Sitka spruce in the Myherin valley near Devils Bridge, 1947.

Harold Wright

were fenced out. So we enjoyed those early stages of the conifer plantations when they looked as innocuous as rows of gooseberry bushes. Years later when we saw them nearing maturity and casting gloom and suffocation across many miles of what had been open moorland we were to lose all love of spruces in the mass.

So I passed a season often with little other company besides that of willow warblers, garden warblers, hedge sparrows, chaffinches, whinchats, yellowhammers, redpolls, pipits, wagtails and sandpipers. I took it all pretty seriously though no one had asked me to do it and I even wrote a paper about it in a scientific journal, *The Naturalist.* This was a north of England publication, for there was little hope of getting anything to do with field studies published in Wales in those days when there was scant Welsh public interest in the natural world.

41

Happily all is now changed. An educational revolution has taken place, bringing environmental and wildlife studies to the fore (the Field Studies Council and a few pioneering schools played their part in this). Today there are plenty of young Welsh people who are first-class field biologists, both amateur and professional, taking part in the conservation of their countryside.

Until the late 1940s I was hardly aware that half a century after the Victorian age there was still a lot of egg-collecting going on. Then in a second-hand shop I picked up a book about birdwatching in south-central Wales, written in the early years of this century. It was, I thought, a delightful piece of writing by a man who so well described his adventures amongst the birds, including an account of how he had fought to save the red kite from extinction. Knowing nothing about this author I assumed him to be dead since his book was then forty years old. But one day I was happy to see an article by him in a bird magazine. So I wrote to him, care of the editor, saying how much I had enjoyed his book, and soon I got a friendly letter from his home in Sussex. Over the next few months we exchanged several amiable letters until I received one that hit me like a bucket of cold water. It was a request that I obtain for him a clutch of Welsh peregrines' eggs which he wanted for a young friend of his who was just starting a collection. It was as much in sadness as disgust that I wrote back telling him what I thought of him. I learned later that his claims to have been a kite protector were completely bogus and that he was in fact one of Britain's most notorious egg thieves. It was a painful experience but a salutory one. After that I was less naive about the wicked ways of collectors.

★   ★   ★

March 25, 1947, was a turning point. I was back from Dale Fort and by now Harold Wright was also married and living in Wales. Following his war service he had become a student in the university college at Aberystwyth. He had brought with him his pre-war plate camera and tripod and his old enthusiasm for getting pictures of birds, and soon we were building photographic hides in secluded places like the Rheidol gorge near Devil's Bridge and, in the following year, in the privacy of the Glanrheidol estate near Aberystwyth.

The Rheidol gorge between Ponterwyd and Devil's Bridge, where we did much of our birdwatching and photography in 1947.

But on this bright March morning in 1947 here we were, cycling up the road from Devil's Bridge towards that stone arch which Johnes of Hafod built over the highway at the top of the hill in 1810 to celebrate the jubilee of poor, mad George III. Prominent on the left up that valley is the farm called Bod-coll and beyond it is a rounded hill over which that day a distant bird was circling. It was a buzzard, yet it was not a buzzard. Its wings were too shapely, its flight more buoyant and its tail was long and forked. Harold, whose sight was always keener than mine, shouted with excitement: 'It's a kite, it's a kite, I tell you!' We looked with awe at this very elegant and at that time ultra-rare raptor which neither of us had ever seen before.

It was not only a new bird for us, it was the beginning of a new chapter in our lives. Until then, though we knew there was still a handful of kites surviving in south-central Wales, we had supposed they were all down in Carmarthenshire, a county unknown to us. We therefore took our kite to be a chance wanderer from the south. But a few weeks later we heard tell of a pair of kites that were nesting not very far from where we had seen our first and we realised that the kite population must be on the move.

Wood warbler, Rheidol gorge, Parson's Bridge, July 1947.

Harold Wright

Wood warbler's nest, Rheidol gorge, Parson's Bridge, 1947.

Harold Wright

Little grebe nesting on a pool at Glanrheidol near Aberystwyth in 1948.

Harold Wright

In due course we heard that Captain and Mrs H. R. H. Vaughan, who lived at Rhandir-mwyn in the beautiful Tywi valley of Carmarthenshire, were proposing to revive the protection of the kite. So one day I cycled from Ponterwyd to Tregaron, then turned east up the steep rough track with several streams to ford (now a metalled road with bridges) that went over the moorlands and down the Tywi to Rhandir-mwyn. From the Vaughans, whom I soon discovered to be totally dedicated conservationists, I learnt that the plight of the kite was truly desperate: it was perhaps still as close to extinction as it had been since the late nineteenth century. So the Kite Committee was formed and one of its crucial first tasks was to find out just how many birds there were—a difficult job in a land of so many valleys and side dingles where little patches of oak woodland, all potential kite breeding places, were folded away in sequestered places.

Sometimes with Harold or other friends, but more often on my own, I spent week after week simply looking for kites. It was a perfect introduction to the wilder hinterland of mid-Wales and to the farmers and shepherds of those hills. Going round the farms and inquiring about kites, I found that I needed various diplomatic skills but what was most useful of all was an ability to drink countless cups of tea and listen to endless tales of a shepherd's life in the uplands. Right from the start the Kite Committee saw that since most kites nested in small woods on sheep farms, the fate of the birds was very much in the hands of the farming community. A key aim has therefore always been to win the support of mid-Wales countryfolk in the cause of kite-protection. That this policy has succeeded is shown by population statistics: only 8 young kites were reared in Wales in 1950 compared with 98 in 1994. So there is good reason to hope that from now on, given continuing protection and the conservation of as many oakwoods as possible, the kite should go on increasing and spreading, a delight to all who look up and marvel at its rich plumage, its gracefulness and its mastery of flight.

Another bird-of-prey comes arrowing across the scene when I think of those years I spent kiting. By the 1940s the merlin was not the bird it had been. From the literature I knew that in parts of Wales it was once fairly common, nesting mainly on heather moors, sometimes in mountain cliffs, quite often in trees, on slopes above the sea or in sand-dunes. Dr Salter of Aberystwyth even found a merlin's nest while he was riding on a local bus. He happened to see the bird slip off her nest in a hawthorn close to the road as the bus rumbled past.

One day I too chanced upon a merlin's nest in a tree. I had been given tea and Welsh cakes at an upland farm and was standing chatting in the farmyard when I heard a thin, agonised shrieking from across the valley. Through my binoculars I could see a merlin, like a tiny peregrine (a male merlin can be smaller than a collared dove), diving repeatedly at two circling buzzards. It happened that I had to go that way and soon here was the merlin again, yickering overhead and throwing himself all over the sky, his blue back occasionally gleaming in the sun. Trees were scattered down the slope below and when I reached the top of a little crag I saw a brown-backed female merlin slide silently out of an old crow's nest in the top of a stunted oak. Through my binoculars I could see two red-brown eggs, just visible through the leaves. As I went away over a shoulder of the hill both merlins raced back and forth above me, shrieking their dislike. Next year I was there again, this time at their courtship season, and I watched them hurtling down the slopes in pursuit of each other at an unbelievable pace, then shooting up high into the sky, then diving again with all the speed of swifts or peregrines.

*   *   *

In the autumn of 1947 Penny and I, at the suggestion of Ronald Lockley, had a complete change of scene. From the wild loneliness of the Plynlimon moorlands we moved to Jersey in the Channel Isles. There we lived by the sea in a house belonging to Ronald and which had been gutted by German troops during the occupation. For months we cared for that stricken house and its brambly wilderness of a garden, gradually restoring them to something like orderliness. We enjoyed Jersey and counted ourselves lucky to have seen it, not in the touristy summer season, but in winter when wild seas raged so often against its cliffs and headlands. Some of the birds were rather special: the Slavonian grebes we often watched diving in the breakers so close to the rocks that we could see the deep, fiery-red of their eyes; the Brent geese guzzling the sea-grass called *Zostera* which lay flat on the wet sand at low tide; the black-throated diver we heard wailing an unseasonable mating song out on the sea; the whimbrels that lived on the seaweedy rocks the winter through. Away from the shore there were the firecrests which often came close as we worked in the garden; the flock of long-tailed tits we saw one day, all with the pure-white heads of the northern continental race. Most precious memory of all is not of a bird but a butterfly: on the autumnal flowers of ivy growing up a wall I saw a large tortoiseshell, still the only one in my life.

Our Christmas Day walk that year was made unique by a cirl bunting singing in a roadside hedge. We had heard the bird frequently all through autumn; but to hear it on December 25 seemed a special benison. Our final memories of Jersey before we left for Wales in mid-March are of carolling woodlarks; mimosas (*Acacia dealbata*) all in yellow flower in mid-February; and the extraordinary dawn-song of a sparrowhawk. This was on March 7 when, the weather being so mild, we slept out in the garden and were woken up at first light by the wailing and yelping of this sparrowhawk in a cypress just over our heads, a solo that went on for half an hour, drowning all other dawn sounds. This virtuoso performance was repeated next morning too. Never since have I heard a sparrowhawk even take part in, let alone dominate, a dawn chorus. Probably it could happen only in March and my dawn-chorus listening since those days has been mostly in May.

In the next two springs, 1948 and 1949, I spent as much time as I could on the lark-singing hills of Cardiganshire. There were not only kites to be located but also other moorland birds about which I still knew so little. I lived three wonderful days in the company of a pair of short-eared owls which had a nest on the ground in a young spruce plantation. I still see their bright-yellow eyes staring deeply into mine from a fence post a few yards away; and I hear a strange clapping together of wings as these beautiful owls of the daylight circled far up in the blue, protesting at my intrusion until they eventually settled down and accepted my hide as part of the scenery.

On an early April day that stays in my mind with special clarity I walked over the moorlands east of Strata Florida looking for the few golden plovers which breed on the mid-Wales uplands. At times it

49

was heavy going as I stumbled over tussocks of moorgrass or floundered across acres of bog-moss, and for the first two hours there was no sign of a golden plover. Then as I passed a lonely tarn a male rose in courtship flight, climbing on strangely slow wings to sing a rather redshank-like ululation, beautiful to hear in that quiet place. But in all the rest of the day I saw only seven other golden plovers though I daresay more than seven saw me as they stood watchful and silent, well camouflaged among clumps of rushes.

I came in late afternoon to a shallow saucer of bogland which the map told me was the source of the Tywi. I found its several springs round the margin of this hollow and from them tiny runnels made their way through rushes, heather and bog-moss to form the infant river. I wanted to go on following its curving gorges down to Rhandir-mwyn but time was against me. The light was fading and I still had to get back to Strata Florida. Nor did I ever manage that walk down the Tywi. I delayed too many years and by the time I might have done it the whole scene had been destroyed by a dreadful reservoir and stifling blocks of conifers.

*　　*　　*

Out of the thirteen pre-1974 counties of Wales the one Penny and I most longed to live in was Merioneth, now better known as Meirionnydd. Much of it is wild and mountainous; except for Cader Idris its peaks are not nearly so visited as those of Eryri further north; many of its rocks are a sufficient mixture of sedimentary and igneous to ensure great variety in the flora. Above all perhaps, except at Blaenau Ffestiniog and along parts of the coast, Meirionnydd has the charm of being sparsely populated. Yet despite our love of the place we have never managed to live there, except very briefly and then it was almost by accident.

After our sojourn on the skirts of Plynlimon above Ponterwyd we had moved down nearer to the coast so that I could read for an M.A. degree at Aberystwyth college. But we were not enjoying village life. We felt a longing for the open spaces and one morning in February, 1950, we got on our cycles and went off for a picnic. We decided, neither of us can remember why, to explore those inviting wooded

50

slopes that climb from the northern shores of the Dyfi estuary and are the southern ramparts of Meirionnydd. We walked up a rough track that zigzagged through the leafless oaks, climbing a few hundred feet until we came clear of the trees. There before us, across a few acres of rocks and dead bracken, was an isolated little whitewashed cottage which looked centuries old and was obviously uninhabited and innocent of any sign of modernity. It was just our sort of dwelling in our sort of place. Spellbound we sat on the step in the clear February sunlight. What a wonderful spot to live in: this air, this view, this solitude! As we sat there entranced, a farmer came by with two sheep-dogs at his heels. The cottage, he said, was looking for a tenant. A month later we arrived with our few bits of furniture and many books, all brought up from the main road by horse and cart, there then being no motorable road to this so desirable residence.

Its place in the world was magnificent. It looked into the sun and its views over the oakwoods and the Dyfi estuary were to the smooth Silurian hills of north Cardiganshire where they fall down to the sea.

Penny at Glygyrog Ddu near Aberdyfi, spring 1950.

It was called Glygyrog Ddu (a corruption of Clegyrog Ddu), a name which to Welsh ears suggests a dwelling amid dark rocks. We moved in March, 1950, on a day when green woodpeckers were bursting with laughter, wailing buzzards plunged and climbed about the sky, pied wagtails chased along the roof-ridge, the year's first wheatear stood brilliant on a sunlit rock and, like a talisman, a woodlark sang his perfect notes standing on our gate post. Clearly we were in for some wonderful days up there amongst the bracken, the gorse, the thickets of blackthorn, the scattered hawthorn trees and the rocks.

We lived through a halcyon spring and summer. It was primitive, much more like camping than house-life. But we were young and didn't suffer from those anxieties about rising damp, uninsulated roofs and draughty windows which make people so miserable as they get towards middle age. Our water supply was a spring a few yards across the sward from our garden gate. As it was overgrown with vegetation we decided to clear it out, discovering in the process that amongst its inhabitants were fifty-two palmate newts. These we returned to the water and we went on sharing the spring with them throughout our stay. The water was delicious. We lived mostly out of doors, making a garden, looking after two hives of bees; and we were as contented as Thoreau by Walden Pond. And like Thoreau in his retreat we had many visitors. They made their way up through the steep oakwoods and some of them brought us new friendships which have lasted all the years since.

Nowhere have we been as blessed with woodlark song as we were at Glygyrog Ddu. Woodlarks were our sparrows. They sang on our chimneys, on our roof, on our fence, on the ground, in the air. Already in March they had a nest with five eggs under a gorse-bush just outside the garden. And they went on singing, sometimes even by night, until midsummer, their company especially precious because the *Handbook of British Birds* told us that the woodlark was 'not in Merioneth'! Redstarts, too, were a happiness. When they came in April and nested in the end wall of the cottage we built a hide of sackcloth and were able to observe these colourful, shy birds at very close range. And we were amused to read in a bird book that redstarts often like to nest in ruins. This seemed a fair description of our new home.

In an ideal world every parish would have its naturalist, someone of long duration in the place, who keeps an eye on the ever-changing woods, fields, streams and their plants and animals; and who faithfully chronicles the events of nature day by day and year by year until the mind dims, the handwriting falters and it is time for a younger scribe to carry on the annals. When Penny and I were living at Glygyrog Ddu our local estuary-side village, Aberdyfi, had just such a Gilbert White who is now remembered only by the oldest inhabitants. We first met E. H. T. Bible in about 1948 and we often went to see him, for he overflowed with reminiscences of local natural history.

Always his great love was the Dyfi estuary. He observed it night and day as the tides streamed by his garden or as he fished for bass from the nearby rocks. There can have been few birds, seals or porpoises that escaped his notice as they made their way up or down the estuary and he faithfully logged them all. Fortunately, many of his observations have been preserved: they can be found in the files of the *Shrewsbury Chronicle* of the twenties and thirties in the 'Nature Notes' column edited by his old friend H. E. Forrest. Some of his diary entries are of real historic value, as when on March 7, 1939, he notes: 'Mr Forrest inquires about mountain hares on Plynlimon. Mr Miall Jones remembers some being released there many years ago.' How fascinating it would be if we could recover the full story of this bringing of mountain hares from presumably Scotland or Ireland to Plynlimon and to learn how long they survived.

Chapter 4

We knew that our idyll above those oak-clad slopes near Aberdyfi could not last. Autumn was coming and I was now teaching in a school on the other side of the estuary. From our hill we could see the school quite clearly through binoculars. It was only two miles away across the salt-marshes and a peregrine could have got there in less than two minutes. But the roads that wind round estuaries are among the longest roads in the world and the thought of cycling fifteen miles in the wind, the rain or the snow was just too daunting. So we returned to Cardiganshire and had the luck to find yet another totally unmodernised, isolated cottage. It was called Felin-y-cwm and was

The old mill cottage, Felin-y-cwm, in Cwm Einion under the slopes of Foel Fawr (1951).   *Harold Wright*

A male redstart, 1951. A pair nested annually in a hole in the wall of Felin-y-cwm.

Harold Wright

hidden away in Cwm Einion, a narrow glen of rocks, bracken, woods and sheep pastures and which English tourists have long known as Artists' Valley.

Felin-y-cwm ('the valley mill') was never itself a mill but a miller's cottage; the mill, now only a dismal ruin, being a few hundred yards upstream. I never saw any millstones lying about but local tradition insists that it was a corn mill. If so, it remembers the day when every farm had its cornfields, its corn buntings and its corncrakes and when the now almost vanished road past the mill was busy with horses and carts loaded with grain. Today what little is left of those crumbling walls ought to be preserved before the site gets altogether lost and forgotten.

55

Female pied flycatcher nesting near Felin-y-cwm, Cwm Einion, 1951.

Harold Wright

The mill cottage lies under the guardianship of a brackeny, heathery hill called Foel Fawr which, though it doesn't reach 900 feet, has a summit of naked rock and manages to look quite mountainy from some angles. When we lived there in the 1950s Foel Fawr was a very special place because of its nightjars, as many as five pairs breeding on our side of the hill alone. They were a delight of still, warm, mothful evenings; and sometimes we slept on the hill for the sake of their company. One of their habits was endearing: often when we came near their domain at dusk a male nightjar would appear from nowhere and flutter close to our faces, hovering for a few seconds like a kestrel and calling *co-ic, co-ic*. Then he would fly away and not come near us again that evening. This gesture of familiarity was no doubt a form of challenge but we liked to think of it as a welcome.

Though these moth-hawks flew only in dusk or darkness we could usually see enough of their movements against the sky to realise what masters of flight they were. They flew fast and silently on their long narrow wings, sometimes patrolling steadily back and forth, sometimes with dragonfly-quick changes of direction. I don't think I have ever been so affected by the beauty of flight as I was by those nightjars of Foel Fawr. The star performance was the full display-flight of the male as he circled in the air clapping his wings or gliding with wings held stiffly high over his back and his tail fanned and depressed right down—an extraordinary posture for any bird to achieve.

Sometimes mystery shrouded our nightjars' way of life. One night the air would be vibrant for hours with their churring and other courtship songs. Yet the very next night, just as warm and still, there might be total silence and no sign of a nightjar anywhere at all, as if the whole community had absconded. The night after, the whole hill would again be throbbing with nightjars. Evidently whatever the difference was between one night and another, it was too subtle for us to appreciate. All we could suppose was that our birds had other feeding grounds besides those on Foel Fawr.

Ring ouzels are a happy memory of Felin-y-cwm. They have always intrigued me because they keep their lives so private up in their heathery solitudes and so often are just an untraceable voice. It

57

was at Felin-y-cwm that I first made the acquaintance of ring ouzels as birds of passage. I found that if I were on the Foel early enough in the morning in the last days of March or early in April I might be lucky enough to see migrant ouzels. My best view was on a late-March morning white with frost. The rising sun had already burnt the hoar off a sizeable patch of turf and there I found nine male ouzels and one female all foraging together. They were very wild and alert but when I stood still against a high wall, they fed down towards me and came close enough for me to see their scale-patterned plumage and their pale wing-bars. When they flew away their flight was swift and direct towards the northern hills, their notes like the *uch-uch-uch-uch* of fieldfares.

One evening in mid-May Penny and I took our sleeping bags up the hill above the cottage and slept among rocks and bracken to discover which bird would be the first to greet Matuta, goddess of the dawn. When we woke at the first pale hint of day, the air was cold and the ground white with frost. A distant nightjar was purring but he fell silent as a wheatear gave us a few spluttering notes against a background of tawny owl hootings. Then came the tremulous, apologetic phrases of a redstart, always one of the first birds to feel the coming light and sing while the dawn is still dark. For nearly half an hour he sang solo until a robin began to tune up along with a distant choir of blackbirds, mistle thrushes, song thrushes and wood-pigeons in the woods below. By five o'clock the dominant voices were chaffinch, wren and both male and female cuckoos. Not until 6.30 on that chilly morning did we hear willow warblers, tree pipits, pied flycatchers and other woodlanders. Strangely, the yellowhammer, usually so very matutinal, did not sing at all and was content with just a few coin-rattling notes.

On a February walk in Cwm Einion our dog—he was a black and white sheep-dog/spaniel cross—began to snuffle with some excitement as he pushed his nose into one of those piles of dead leaves that are gathered by the wind in draughty, sheep-grazed woods. He almost disappeared into that heap and when he came out he held in his mouth, quite unharmed, a yellow-brown, furry mouse with large eyes, prominent ears and a bushy tail. It was the first dormouse I had ever seen and the first time I realised there were any dormice in the district. As this mouse showed no fear I took it back to the cottage where it immediately ate most of two large raisins. Then it went to sleep and did not reawaken until the following afternoon when it ate a raisin and a walnut, drank a little water and went back to sleep again. That night there was a hard frost and next day the dormouse remained asleep. So I took him back to his haven of leaves to sleep away the rest of the winter.

My next encounter with a dormouse came a year and a half later. I was in front of my class in the schoolroom one sunny July morning when the lesson was interrupted by a boy who, evidently bored by '*amo, amas, amat*', looked out of the window and suddenly shrieked: 'Sir, there's a baby squirrel!' It was well known that Sir could easily be distracted from Latin verbs by an intrusion of natural history. So for a while our progress towards perfection in the language of the Caesars was forgotten in favour of observing this 'baby squirrel' which was in fact a dormouse creeping about the twigs of a honeysuckle bush and nibbling at the long slender tubes of the flowers, no doubt for their nectar. This happy interlude gave me the chance to explain to the class that they were witnessing something rather rare—a mainly nocturnal animal venturing out in broad daylight. I wonder if, after forty years, any of them remember that pretty scene? One thing is sure: the dormice are still there. Nest boxes put up on trees for the birds are quite frequently occupied by dormice, sometimes for breeding, sometimes for hibernation.

⋆   ⋆   ⋆

Pearl-bordered fritillaries in great abundance are a colourful memory of our days in Cwm Einion but I need to go back a few years earlier to begin the story at the beginning. In the summer of 1947 when Penny and I were living in our hill cottage above Ponterwyd we were called on one day by two strangers who introduced themselves as Frank Best and Arthur Cadman of the Forestry Commission. They knew about us because we had applied for a permit to carry out bird surveys in the Commission's plantations. In recent years they had planned the new Hafren Forest, a vast spread of conifers on the east side of Plynlimon. Now they were working to the south side in the

Small pearl-bordered fritillary, one of a communal roost at Felin-y-cwm, Cwm Einion.

Myherin and Rhuddnant valleys, near Devil's Bridge. They were not only foresters but keen all-round naturalists who became our friends from that day on.

Frank Best was especially good at butterflies and he occasionally called on us when, a few years later, we were living in Cwm Einion. It was on one of these visits that he showed us how to distinguish between the pearl-bordered and the small pearl-bordered fritillaries. There could have been no better place to learn about these engaging creatures because at that time our little Felin-y-cwm garden was full of them for a few weeks every spring, being perfectly positioned for both species: it lay between the woodland habitat of the pearl-bordered fritillary and the moorlands preferred by the small pearl-bordered. From late April or early May till late June these little orange butterflies fluttered abundantly on our patches of purple aubretia but it wasn't until Frank Best sorted them out for us that we realised that it was the pearl-bordered which came first. Then after a couple of weeks or so they were joined by the very similar small pearl-bordered. These newcomers, despite their name, did not look any smaller but could be distinguished with a bit of practice by the pattern of their underwing. Little did we appreciate then how privileged we were to have both these butterflies side by side and in such abundance. In only a few years the pearl-bordered had quite gone from the valley as they have from many other places, leaving only the small pearl-bordered to cheer us on our way.

An endearing habit of the small pearl-bordered fritillaries was that they roosted communally. Just outside the garden was a patch of rushes and the butterflies (forty-six was the most we ever saw) would gather there at sunset, each spending the night clinging to a dead, brown seed-head which they resembled very closely when their wings were closed. But before they went to sleep, there were a magical few minutes when they clung to the rushes with their wings wide open to catch the last rays of the sun. In the morning there was a similar scene of delight: as the rising sun reached them, they opened their wings and held that position fifteen or twenty minutes until one by one they warmed up and flew away. After these little fritillaries of the spring our garden at Felin-y-cwm occasionally attracted those bigger, more dashing, difficult-to-interview fritillaries: the silver-washed, the dark-green and the high brown. Sad to report, the high brown, always the rarest, has now vanished from the valley as completely as the pearl-bordered; and the silver-washed is also in decline.

Snails were a feature of Felin-y-cwm garden, the big common snails which so heartily devoured our lettuces and cabbages. I would not kill them. Instead I went after dark with a torch and gathered them in a bucket which I emptied in the wood on the other side of the river. But such was their passion for reproduction that our snails never got fewer no matter how many I sent into exile. Their multitudes just there were of ecological interest. On the whole this district of limeless soils belongs emphatically to slugs rather than snails because snails need lime to make their shells. So it seems likely that a band of calcium-rich rock goes across the valley thereabouts. Lime-loving plants in the wood below the garden—sanicle, yellow archangel and dog's mercury—tell the same story as the snails. So do the many ash trees and the small-leaved limes.

In recent years otters have been in the news because of their decline, even their total disappearance, in many districts. So far in this part of Wales we have been fortunate; we still have otters though I daresay they are fewer than half a century ago. Certainly they are extremely elusive and you need the luck of Old Harry even to get a glimpse of one. Penny and I lived at Felin-y-cwm within sound of the river for eight years and never saw an otter though occasionally we heard them whistling as they moved up and down the valley at night. Yet when a niece of ours stayed with us one weekend, she and a friend strolled down to the river and what do they see but an otter come boldly out of the water to perch on a midstream rock! Since those days, though I have twice seen an otter by day on the Dyfi estuary, I still have not seen one in Cwm Einion.

When people have asked me why I left the Midlands for Wales they have given me an odd look when I've told them it was so that I could have buzzards as my neighbours. The great, floating, circling, wailing buzzards—the eagles of Wales—are as good a symbol as any of the wilder Britain that has so shrunken with the centuries. For many years they were only spring and summer birds for me—holiday birds—and it was not until we went to live amongst them in the woodlands of Cwm Einion that I began to learn a little about their winter life. Till then I had supposed that they were mindful of their nests only in the breeding season. But I soon realised that some pairs of buzzards keep an eye on their nest at all seasons.

Across the cwm, a little upstream from our cottage, was an abandoned slate quarry, a quiet, mysterious place deeply shadowed. Here on a ledge a pair of buzzards nested year after year; and from time to time, even in December and January, we heard excited yelpings and cat-calls coming from our quarry buzzards. Clearly these sporadic visits to their nest-site were an important link in their pair-bond; and sometimes, also in the depths of winter, both birds would circle and call or dive and zoom with all the *brio* of an April morning, especially if a stimulating cold wind filled the valley from the north-west.

As their big stick nest, the accumulation of several seasons, could easily be peeped into from the lip of the quarry I could see the evidence of their visits: the nest was kept tidy and neatly hollowed and sometimes green garlands of ivy were left on it like religious offerings. It was not only that nest they decorated: as if to keep their options open they brought similar greenery to another old nest of theirs in a small-leaved lime tree close to our cottage. One year, in the last week of February, I experimented to find out how active their house-keeping was on their ledge in the quarry. On several successive days I dropped a pile of sticks onto the nest and on each day, when I checked a few hours later, I found that my sticks had been tidied up and placed round the edge of the nest.

There was something else to be learnt about the winter life of buzzards. They are not always the 'birds of lazy flight' the books so often talk about. Maybe in summer, when food is abundant, they can take their time over hunting; but in hungry winters they can dash after their prey like goshawks. One day, as I crossed the Einion on the foot-bridge below Felin-y-cwm, a wood-pigeon came hurtling down the valley followed a few feet behind by just as headlong a buzzard. Pursued and pursuer quickly vanished round a bend in the stream and I missed the end of the chase. But things did not look good for that pigeon.

Occasionally I have known buzzards that were very aggressive towards people. Walking one day with my dog I passed near a buzzard's nest high in a hedgerow tree. The dog, running on ahead, was dived at with a threatening swoosh of wings and a few moments later I received the same treatment. The buzzard did not strike me but he came repeatedly to within a few inches of my head. For the next few days I got a similar reception every time I crossed that field. But my dog refused to follow me. Instead he went all round the field, keeping to the shelter of the hedge.

You won't go far in buzzard country before you see the local carrion crows at one of their favourite pastimes, which might be described as 'buzzard bashing', in which a crow or several crows make a great show of harassing a flying buzzard by diving at it repeatedly. The buzzard either ignores these insults or turns momentarily on its back and shoots out a threatening talon. Since it is rare to see a buzzard chasing a crow I wondered at first why crows were all so passionately anti-buzzard. I soon learnt why when I began to examine buzzards' eyries in June and July when the young were nearly ready to fly. There was no mistaking what some broods were mainly fed on: the edges of the nests were often black with the feathers of young crows. And one day I was able to watch a pair of buzzards repeatedly raid a crow's nest and carry off the young despite being mobbed by every crow in the district.

There is no doubt about what is my strangest experience with buzzards. I am on a hillside in mid-April looking down on a rookery and enjoying the massed choir of rook voices when, to my astonishment, two buzzards come power-diving out of the sky side by side to land on a rook's nest right in the heart of the rookery amid a clamour of outraged rooks. I assume the buzzards are a raiding party out to snatch a young rook or two. But I am wrong. For several minutes they lie fluttering in the nest and through binoculars I can see that they are mating. Then they fly away quite nonchalantly despite being chivvied by every rook in the commune. I am left marvelling that they chose such a freakish spot for their amours. Why not their own nest, I wonder.

*   *   *

Twice in my life, unhappily, I have exchanged red squirrels for greys, first in the Worcestershire woods of the 1930s and again when I came to live in Wales. In the Einion valley in 1950 the greys, though threatening from east and south, were still far away, or so we thought. And the reds were an attractive feature of our daily walks, interesting for everything they did, their eating, their pairing and their nest-building. They usually made no secret about where they were building their homes, openly carrying great mouthfuls of materials though we watched from only a few paces away. They worked hard building footballs of moss and soft twigs in the crowns of small trees. When I climbed up to inspect these dreys I found that, despite their rough exteriors, they were beautifully fashioned inside into a warm and comfortable room that was reached by a well-constructed tunnel. Some nests had more than one entrance and several had ingenious flaps which hung down to curtain the doorway.

Those red squirrels changed remarkably from winter to summer. In winter (the pairing season) their fur was at its best—a thick protection against the cold and often quite a sombre grey-brown rather than red. Their ears were then sharply crowned with prominent tufts. Their tails were full and bushy and usually a rich dark-red; and once I noted a tail as 'practically black'. As spring went by, the body fur became thinner and much redder while the ear tufts got smaller or disappeared completely, so robbing the squirrels of that appealing perky look that makes them popular subjects for Christmas cards. At the same time the tail faded, beginning at the tip, and for a while some squirrels looked quite bizarre, with tails half-dark, half-pale. The final colour of the tail, reached in May, was a light-straw which in bright sun could appear almost white.

We had been living in Cwm Einion two years when the first grey squirrel was recorded in the parish, seen by Hubert Mappin on his great lawn at Ynys-hir just before Christmas, 1952. For the next few years grey squirrels were seen only at rare intervals. Then quite abruptly in 1961 they were being reported all over north Cardiganshire, even one on the promenade at Aberystwyth. On June 16, 1963, I saw a red squirrel in some pines near the estuary. Optimistically I wrote in my diary: 'It is the third here this week, so maybe they are increasing'. It was the last I ever saw in the parish. Strangely I cannot remember whether our red squirrels were noisy or not; but certainly our grey squirrels offend our ears very often. Most voices in nature, even the outlandish ones, at least have the merit of being startling or intriguing or amusing. But the grouchy, grumpy, growlings of grey squirrels achieve a rare degree of unattractiveness.

*   *   *

There was a time when Harold Wright and I had a little rowing boat that we used for a special sort of estuary birdwatching. The trick was always to go with the tide whichever way it was running. Sometimes it floated us inland for a mile or so until the turn of the tide brought us back home again—a slow journey on placid waters. To go downstream on a receding high tide was much more of an adventure, especially where the estuary widens at its mouth and we could see white waves breaking over the bar not far ahead. We shall never know why that great sheet of quickly moving water never swept our eggshell of a boat past the safe haven of Aberdyfi and out to sea.

The marvel of those ebb-tide frolics was that we could get so close to the estuary's wildest birds, for they have such little fear of boats that it was possible to drift in amongst rafts of teal and wigeon, provided we lay flat and peeped very carefully over the side. No doubt the ducks took us for just another heap of debris like so many carried up and down the estuary with the tides. Even more exciting to us were the waders which we normally knew only as voices across the mudflats and which we seldom saw except in distant flight, for there were no hides at the side of the estuary in those days. In our flat-bottomed craft we slid past ranks of grey plovers, godwits, spotted redshanks, curlews and oystercatchers at only a few feet range. So we learnt how exquisite are the plumages of all waders when seen in close-up detail. Over half a century later we both still vividly remember the day we saw a large bird battling towards us against the estuary wind. At first we thought it was a heron and then to our amazement it dived into the water with a big splash and flew away, fish in talon. Birdwatchers never forget their first osprey.

*   *   *

These days what used to be the moorland head of Cwm Einion is dense with tall plantations of spruce and larch and some blocks have already been clear-felled. But when Harold and I began birdwatching there in about 1950 the trees had reached no more than ten or twelve feet. They had passed through the shrubbery stage when they had doubtless been breeding places for hedge sparrows, garden warblers and other bush nesters, and now they had reached the height when they became ideal for lesser redpolls. Ever since our days in the Myherin valley we had been especially interested in redpolls and now in Cwm Einion we found more of their nests and built hides close to them, for they are fearless little birds and there was no danger of disturbing them.

A quirk we detected in their behaviour was that there were occasionally triangular relationships among them, made up of one male and two females. By this I don't mean bigamy. In the redpoll triangles that we observed the two hens did not have a nest each but joined forces to build one nest only. One female alone was mated to the male redpoll, the other acting as a servant. The mated hen did all the incubating but was fed by the cock bird and the other hen; and as she sat on the nest she made the same wing-quivering, food-begging displays to both. The young were fed by both the mother and the servant but if mother and servant happened to arrive at the nest together the servant fed the mother who then regurgitated the food to give it to the young. Though not bigamous, this triangle was an emotionally involved relationship: during courtship the male displayed to both his mate and to the servant, then all three would go off on wild flights together above the little spruces. And what are we to make of the pair we watched diligently building a nest and then taking it apart and rebuilding it in a similar spruce a few yards away?

When I look back on the eight years of the 1950s when Penny and I lived in Cwm Einion I see a kaleidoscope of many small images that crowd in on each other in total lack of order. Perhaps I lie awake at night and remember the glow-worms that shone their green lamps along the laneside up the Foel. Or the heaving piles of animation that were the wood ants' nests near Furnace Falls; or the big beetle I found on the Foel one day: it had a grossly distended body and very small wing cases and from a book I identified it as an oil beetle, an insect I have seen nowhere else. Or I remember the balsam poplar we planted at Felin-y-cwm to scent the air in spring and were delighted to find it soon became a home for poplar hawkmoth caterpillars as well as the strangely humped caterpillars of the pebble prominent moth.

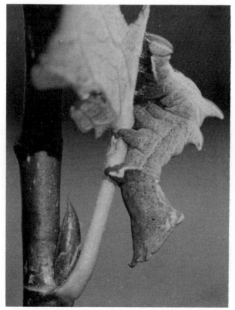

The curiously humped caterpillar of the pebble prominent moth feeding on balsam poplar leaves at Felin-y-cwm.

Or I think of the great moth that one night came tapping on our lamp-lit window under which Penny had planted a fragrance of night-scented tobacco flowers: it was the only convolvulus hawkmoth we have ever seen alive. Yellow butterflies are also memories of those days of the fifties. They were brimstones and were very dear to us because, though this is such a common butterfly of more southern districts, it was always rare hereabouts. Yet nearly every year, spring or autumn, we used to see them in our Felin-y-cwm garden. And just outside our gate there was a very special birch tree. There are hundreds of birches in Cwm Einion but this one was honeycombed near its base with the tunnels of goatmoth caterpillars which gave off a scent attractive to butterflies. Sometimes we saw a score or so of red admirals clustered on the trunk of that one birch. The slopes above our cottage in spring were the place to find those curiously local, stay-at-home butterflies, the green hairstreaks. On the wing they could easily be mistaken for little brown leaves tossed away by the wind. But when settled and slanting their green underwings to take the sunlight they scintillated like some butterfly of the tropics.

The patience of insects is something to marvel at. I kept my eye on a scarlet tiger-moth during a wet week in June. When the rain began this moth crawled under a leaf of a shrub in the garden; and there it remained quite motionless until the sun shone again six days later. So it must be with countless insects all around us when it rains in summer, each of them waiting in the shelter of a leaf or some other little roof. But how many of them are we aware of?

Vignettes of birds also come to mind and if I had but a smidgeon of artistic ability I would have loved to sketch them for the margins of these pages. There were the thirty or so snow buntings, dressed all in white, which one winter's day appeared from nowhere and flew tinkling their little bells down the valley past our cottage, never to be seen by us again. I think of the long-tailed tits' nest we found in a briar of wild rose behind the cottage before the end of winter: already half-built it must have been started in early February, so slowly do these birdlets put together their complicated balls of moss, wool and lichen fragments.

A marvel of flight was that of a pair of stock doves which nested in the ruined walls of our local lead-mine. Sometimes I went there with no other purpose than to sit on the hill above the mine and watch the graceful ballet of their aerial courtship, circling and sweeping about the sky, side by side or closely behind one another, sometimes moving at headlong speed, sometimes with strange slow-motion wing-beats or gliding gently with wings partly closed. In dull light they were a nondescript grey. In bright sun and at certain angles a wonderful blue sheen transformed them, especially when there was also a flash of green off the sides of their necks.

A crow struggles against the wind with a long stick across her beak. The stick hangs lop-sided and awkward and to improve her control of it she deftly transfers it to her claws in mid-air and quickly back to her beak and so gets it better balanced. A pair of ravens have built a nest on the outskirts of a rookery as they do occasionally. Seeing me, the male raven flies wildly back and forth over the wood, calling in anger. He longs to attack me but dare not. Instead he dives onto a rook in mid-air. The blow is loud enough for me to hear it but the rook merely drops a few feet, sheds a feather or two and then goes on as if this is a daily occurrence. A male kestrel, red-backed and blue-headed, is hovering. A flock of starlings, in a long, sideways-strung line, comes hastening across the field below him. As if at a word of command, as they come underneath the kestrel their ranks close; so that when they are immediately below him they form a solid ball of starlings which spreads out again as soon as the kestrel is passed, the whole remarkable performance being accomplished without any loss of speed. Thought transference or what?

Chapter 5

I have two regrets about my visits to the Aberystwyth district in the late 1930s. One was that I never met John Henry Salter, the outstanding local naturalist of his day. I had his book, *The Flowering Plants and Ferns of Cardiganshire* (1935), but knew nothing of the Quakerly man himself. He died in 1942 but he lives on through his published works and in his multi-volumed manuscript diary which is in the National Library of Wales and is a monumental record of a lifetime devoted to the observation not only of wild plants but also of garden plants, birds (he was a pioneer kite conservationist), mammals and insects.

Ringed plover, Ynys-las, 1947.

Harold Wright

Red Kite, now increasing in Britain after being almost exterminated.

Our dog found this dormouse asleep in a pile of dead leaves in Cwm Einion.

Stumps of prehistoric trees at low tide at Borth, Cardiganshire, c. 1960.

Ynys Enlli (Bardsey Island).

My other regret is that I never made a pre-war visit to the mouth of the Dyfi at Ynys-las. From what I was able to glean later from naturalists who knew Ynys-las before 1939, it was a quiet, remote place visited by very few holiday-makers and then mostly in August. All through spring the breeding shore birds were blissfully undisturbed, their chief danger being the occasional extra-high tides. Along with many pairs of ringed plovers and oystercatchers there was a thriving population of little terns. Nightjars and merlins nested annually in the dunes. 1939 destroyed the idyll. In came the military, the estuary was turned into a practice range for rockets and most of the breeding birds disappeared for ever. When Penny and I first got there just after the war there was a mess of abandoned military buildings and concrete gun emplacements; and at low tide the estuary towards Glandyfi was a forest of spent rockets sticking grotesquely out of the mud and all leaning towards the west from where they had been fired.

In the early 1950s we camped several times in the dunes and if it were spring we invariably had the whole place to ourselves. Spring or summer we rejoiced in the dune wildflowers: thyme, violets, sea holly, the spurges, hound's-tongue, pyramidal orchid, the many colourful marsh orchids and the patches of rest-harrow which give a special pungent flavour to the air of dunes. In his flora Salter had noted that although there were bee orchids only a mile away across the estuary at Aberdyfi dunes there were none at Ynys-las. By the time Penny and I got to Ynys-las in 1951, the bee orchid had arrived though it was getting very rough treatment from a monstrous regiment of rabbits. Then 1954 brought myxomatosis and next year it was a joy to go to the dunes in late January and find the young leaves of the bee orchids untouched by any nibbling; and in the summer to see plenty of bee orchids all in flower, a splendour which lessened in subsequent years as the rabbits came back.

Ynys-las dunes no longer resemble some wild fragment of the Gobi Desert. Now they are a National Nature Reserve with car-park, visitor centre, shop, ice-cream stall, toilets, boardwalks, railings and notice-boards. Not that I'm complaining: if they were not a nature reserve the lovely dunes would by now have been ruined one way or another by exploiters or by being trampled into squalor. Instead they remain comparatively unspoilt, their flora and other wildlife still

71

Cors Fochno, the peatbog National Nature Reserve near Borth, north Cardiganshire.

largely intact. Like all such reserves, these beautiful but fragile dunes offer refreshment for the human spirit and are a place where many people can come and learn about the world of nature and why it must be protected wherever possible. It may be well to remember that this duneland oasis was not created by the waving of a wand but by a long struggle by conservationists against objectors and philistines—the story of nature reserves and national parks the world over.

Close to Ynys-las dunes is the great undrained peatbog, Cors Fochno, a National Nature Reserve lying inland of the coastal village of Borth. It was early in the 1950s that I began to get acquainted with this soggy, prehistoric wilderness that is such an improbable survival in the modern world. One of the best views of it is from just north of Tal-y-bont on A487, the Aberystwyth-Machynlleth road. But I can't pretend that on a dull winter's day it is a landscape that will appeal to everyone—it looks too much like the desolate Egdon Heath of Hardy's novels: the sort of barren waste where you can imagine the last surviving aurochs might have lingered until it sank to its death in some bottomless quag.

This bog of Cors Fochno looks quite different on a fine day when the cloud shadows are chasing across and the vegetation is coloured with bands of dark-red, tawny, gold, green or russet according to the season or the time of day. There can also be wonderful effects as the evening light begins to flood in and the setting sun reddens the waters of Cardigan Bay. Then the whole miry plain may seem strangely luminous, becoming one with the sea and reaching away to infinity.

In the 1950s the bog had another attraction: it was the winter feeding ground of a flock of white-fronted geese, which was why I first went there. In February 1954, Arthur Cadman, who knew more than anyone about our local wildfowl, had been told that six hundred geese had been seen on the bog and he was anxious to check on this figure since it was far in excess of usual counts. I went with him on an oozy plod across this tremulous mire, feeling all the time that we were treading on a very thin skin stretched precariously over watery depths. For a long way we saw nothing and then (to our shame), before we realised they were there, a multitude of geese rose from the centre of the bog with a clangour of exciting cries. From their many droppings we could see they had been feeding on shoots of cross-leaved heath and we also found a patch of cotton-grass which had been pulled up so that its roots could be eaten. Seeing their peatbog habitat, their very dark plumage and their yellow bills, Arthur Cadman declared them to be Greenland whitefronts though until then this race had not been recorded in the Borth-Dyfi area.

This wilderness behind Borth was long a place of controversy. On the one hand were the farmers who, following the traditions of centuries, wanted it drained and turned into agricultural land. Opposed to them were the conservationists for whom Cors Fochno was a cherished last refuge of ever decreasing plants and animals. It was also treasured as a storehouse of knowledge because in its depths (there are twenty-three feet of peat at the centre) is preserved in neat order of time the still identifiable pollen that has blown there from the trees of thousands of years. So Borth Bog has a unique story to tell about the history and prehistory of our local forests. It is a window on the past and is a present-day haven for bladderworts, sundews, bog rosemary and white beak-sedge; large heath and other butterflies;

frogs, toads and adders; wildfowl, short-eared owls and harriers. And who knows what else?

For Penny and me Ynys-las dunes and Borth Bog were our introduction to coastal Cardiganshire. We swam at Borth at high tide and stubbed our toes against the stumps of trees that are still rooted where they grew thousands of years ago, before the sea invaded the now lost land which the medieval story-tellers called Cantref y Gwaelod ('the Lowland Hundred'). In winter we walked the cliffs from Borth to Aberystwyth and watched choughs and peregrines and saw rafts of black scoters on the sea. We walked there in spring as well and met with migrant wheatears, warblers and occasional ring ouzels.

The town of Aberystwyth, we soon learned, had two special birds in winter. One, very elusive, was the black redstart; the other, easy to see, was the purple sandpiper. The black redstart has long been known to pass the winter in very small numbers along the coast of Wales, especially in south-west Pembrokeshire. Its sojourns at Aberystwyth have, it seems, always been sporadic. It would come there several winters in succession, then there would be many years of near absence. 1947-50 was a good period when, autumn to spring, we quite often saw black redstarts in various parts of the town but mostly on or near the sea-front. They were invariably chance meetings: we would happen to look up at the castle ruins or the old college buildings and see a little dark bird with a fiery tail fluttering out to take insects in the air. Occasionally we saw them round the harbour but our best views were when they perched on the gravestones (now removed, alas) in St Michael's churchyard, next-door to the castle ruins.

Because it faces so many Irish Sea gales, Aberystwyth has had to provide itself with a massive wall against the waves, a wall faced with knobbly blocks of granite. They are useful, those knobs. At high water purple sandpipers perch on them, waiting for the tide to ebb so that they can go back to the seaweedy rocks where they feed. I had visited Aberystwyth many times before I became aware of these little, dark-brown waders. (You need to get very close in bright light if you are going to catch the purple sheen that sometimes flashes off their feathers.) One April day I was walking along the promenade and happened to lean over the rail and there a few feet below, were thirteen purple sandpipers on the face of the wall. They kept up a musical conversation and seemed rather excited, perhaps at the thought that they would very soon be leaving for their arctic breeding grounds. Every few minutes, when an extra-large wave came washing up the wall, they leapt into the air like dancers and immediately settled again.

Their devotion to that wall is extraordinary. There they are day after day at high tide all through from autumn to spring. Yet they are scarce elsewhere on this part of the coast. Strangely, although these sandpipers may feed daily with turnstones, redshanks and ringed plovers, these other waders hardly ever come to share the sandpipers' high-tide roost. Records of the purple sandpiper using the wall go back many decades and maybe the habit began even in the wall's very first autumn after, as a plaque on the promenade informs us, 'the last stone of this wall was laid by Councillor Evan Hugh James, the Mayor, on the 4th day of July, 1903'.

★   ★   ★

In 1952 we bought our first car, a 1936 Austin Seven and the days of our innocence were over. From then on we laid aside our bicycles and became ozone-unfriendly contributors to global warming, wasters of fossil fuels, polluters of the country air, makers of unnecessary noise and a threat to birds and hedgehogs. But no such dismal ideas then clouded our minds as we went joyously off to explore the Cardiganshire coast in our chugging little rag-top car. On steep slopes above the cliffs, seven miles south of Aberystwyth, we saw oakwoods that are amongst the most ancient and least interfered with woods in the whole of Wales. With total improbability they flourish in the salty sting of the ocean gales which have pruned them to the size of dwarves. Yet though they seem to belong as much to the sea as to the land, we found that these woods have many of the normal oakwood wildflowers—anemone, wood sorrel, lords and ladies, enchanter's nightshade and dog's mercury. Mercifully these primitive woods are now in the care of the Dyfed Wildlife Trust—its Penderi reserve.

On a summer evening in 1954 I went off with my sleeping bag to New Quay Head where I had been told was Cardiganshire's major

75

seabird colony. I slept amongst the cliff-top gorse and woke to the calls and flutterings of stonechats, linnets and whitethroats that were feeding their young all round. Quite unaware of me lying there, a family of choughs—the young distinguishable by their yellow, not red, beaks—were foraging on the nearby sward, the closest I have ever been to these elegant fowl. The cliffs, I found, fell sheer into deep water even at low tide and were home for a sizeable community of razorbills, guillemots and herring gulls with smaller numbers of cormorants and shags. A fulmar patrolling the cliffs was still a notable bird at that time, as it was only seven years since the first pair had nested there. Of kittiwakes there was no sign at all, for the colony breeding there now did not begin to assemble for another eight years.

I treasure a quite different memory of New Quay. One chilly spring day there was only one other figure on the beach besides myself and when we got into conversation I found he was an Irish labourer working on a farm near Cardigan. He had cycled twenty miles that sunny Saturday afternoon for he had heard that New Quay was 'a place with a very foine strand'. Now he was here he agreed it was so but he assured me that there was also 'some foine country around Cork City, bedad'. He was delighted when I told him I longed to go to Cork because I believed some of my ancestors hailed from there. As he got on his bike to cycle back to Cardigan he heaped blessings on me as only the Irish can and said he very much hoped we would meet again. We never did, of course, and what's more, I still have not got to Cork. Instead it reposes in my mind as a far-away, dreamed-of Nirvana.

As time went by Penny and I got acquainted with the most southern parts of Cardigan's beautiful coast. On a rare hot day in mid-May we turned off the main road down a coastward lane that narrowed as the sea got near. We passed through a hamlet with a wonderful name—Llandysiliogogo—and then as the hedges began to touch overhead, the way dropped steep and winding into a wooded glen where we were away from heat, glare and dust by a sycamore-darkened stream. Here was a cool, green light. Everywhere there were bluebells and hart's tongue ferns. And the spring-like weather had brought out the pearl-bordered fritillaries, richly orange in their first-day freshness.

We walked across the clean-washed pebbles of the narrow cove at Cwmtudu which is hemmed in by distorted and crumpled cliffs that are hollowed by caves. We could now turn north-east up the coast or south-west towards Lochdyn. We chose Lochdyn because we had heard that there the land hooked right round and pointed north into the sea to end in a high-tide island. We scrambled up a grassy bank patched white with scurvy-grass. A pair of rock pipits, carrying food in their beaks, shrieked at us with dislike. When we peeped over the cliff a startled whimbrel cried loudly as it flew out to sea. There was a sweet fragrance of thrift and a not-so-sweet odour of gulls' nesting ledges. We followed the cliff slopes on a precarious sheep-track which got us through rainforest-like thickets of bramble and wild privet. Far below we could see grey seals lying out on flat, water-encircled rocks, sprawling with the abandon that only seals can achieve, lying on their backs, their tails and flippers in the air. The whole herd looked as if it had been washed up and left to die by the last tide. It was such a still day we could hear the rustle of a cormorant's wings as he hurried by; and we could catch every syllable of conversation from herring gulls floating on the glass-smooth sea though they were invisible behind a heat haze that lay across the water.

From the bracken a face watched us, a red-brown face with sharp ears and a white mouth—one of the many foxes of those cliffs. As he leapt away two ravens stooped and barked at him from the air; and out on the water the gulls, hearing the anger of the ravens, wailed almost like great northern divers. By now our walk had degenerated into a hopeless struggle with gorse and waist-deep heather. We were thankful to reach what was obviously a badgers' path which led us straight up and out of the jungle. At the top we turned for home. Though Lochdyn was not to be reached that day we went there often in the years that followed and are happy to think that so much of that lovely coast is now safe in the hands of the National Trust. Just imagine what horrors the philistines of tourism would have achieved if they could have got that perfect shore into their clutches!

From the most southern of Ceredigion's cliffs, those that reach out closest to Cardigan Island, a small flower and a small bird stay ever in my mind. The carpets of vernal squill were bluer there and more extensive than I have known them anywhere else. And there were the house martins. Back in Gwbert village I had seen martins squabbling vulgarly with sparrows about who owned a nest under the eaves of a house. But a mile round the coast a pair of martins were quite alone at their nest by a clump of bright-green sea spleenwort under the eaves of the cliffs. I felt that this was where martins ought to be, occupying their primeval place in the world amid these huge surroundings of rock and water, looking no bigger than insects as the sea winds hurled them about in the spray-filled air.

★   ★   ★

Exploring inland Cardiganshire I came to Hafod Uchdryd, a twice-blest spot because rich in both natural and human history. Long neglected, this once sumptuous estate deep in the valley of the upper Ystwyth was reverting to the wild and had become a refuge for ravens and birds of prey which nested in the woods of beech and oak, or what was left of them after the devastation of the Second World War. (I have a dismal earlier memory of cycling down the hill past Hafod during the first few years of the war and seeing its oakwoods in the process of being destroyed.) Like most people I first got to know Hafod's human story by reading *Peacocks in Paradise* in which Elizabeth Inglis-Jones relates the Romantic (in the true sense) saga of that strange man Thomas Johnes who came to this fair vale and built himself a Gothic mansion complete with a library full of precious manuscripts. He made gardens, grottoes, walks, waterfalls. He pioneered agriculture. He planted trees all over the surrounding hills. Dearer to his heart than almost anything, he made translations of tales of chivalry from medieval French chronicles. He even installed a printing press for the production of his works.

When I first saw Hafod house it was forlorn and deserted but it still had elements of melancholy beauty, a tall campanile giving a touch of elegance. But in came the demolition agents who stripped away anything of value and what was left was a ruin loud with jackdaws. By then the whole property had been acquired by the Forestry Commission and they decided to raze the now roofless mansion to the ground because it had become a danger 'inviting amateur rock-climbing exercises by foolhardy undergraduates from the university

The gutted remains of Hafod Uchdryd house just before final demolition in 1958.

at Aberystwyth'. So it came about that in August 1958, 230 sticks of gelignite demolished what was left of Hafod house. As George Ryle put it in his book *Forest Service*: 'When a second shot was fired to complete the demolition, out from the topmost chimney, calm and unhurried, drifted a fine old barn owl; and away over the hills went the ghost of Hafod'. So was thrown away a piece of Cardiganshire's history. No doubt if the proposal to obliterate this historic house had come thirty years later there would have been a huge public outcry that would have saved it. As things were in 1958, though there were protests, they were not organised into a chorus powerful enough to carry the day.

Among the annals of Hafod, naturalists especially cherish the visits there in the 1790s of Dr James Edward Smith who, a few years earlier, had founded the Linnaean Society. Smith, still only in his thirties, was already one of Britain's most distinguished naturalists.

He was totally charmed by Hafod and was impressed by the knowledge of plants and animals displayed by eleven-year-old Mariamne, Johnes's much-loved daughter. It was to her that Smith's *Natural History of the rarer Lepidopterous Insects of Georgia* was dedicated. With Sowerby as illustrator, Smith became the author of a monumental *English Botany* in thirty-six volumes, a work that comes into the Hafod story because some of its illustrations show lichens which were collected there. (The specimens still survive in herbaria.) Poor Smith. It is well that he did not live to see that his great work was destined to be known by all succeeding generations as '*Sowerby's English Botany*'.

When I think back to my earliest visits to Hafod I see the wide swards in front of the house being kept short by sheep and by an odd-looking circus of rabbits, not only ordinary brown rabbits but also black ones, white ones, pied ones and even some that were all-yellow or black and yellow; a colourful population that I suppose might have gone on until today if myxomatosis had not struck in the mid-1950s. A final memory I cherish is of going to the village school at Devil's Bridge to hear Elizabeth Inglis-Jones talk about *Peacocks in Paradise* and how she came to write that charming book. For all who heard her that evening Hafod lived again.

The Hafod saga is inseparable from that of another now demolished mansion, Dolaucothi, twenty miles south-west. For here lived Thomas Johnes's beautiful cousin Jane, whom he married around the time he acquired Hafod. For a long period Dolaucothi wielded power over large estates but the twentieth century brought severe financial decline and the house eventually fell into disuse. When Penny and I think of Dolaucothi we remember a letter we received in about 1948 from Ronald Lockley as chairman of the West Wales Field Society (now the Dyfed Wildlife Trust). Ronald, ever a man of schemes and dreams, wrote that the Society was seriously thinking of buying Dolaucothi. And if they succeeded, would Penny and I go and live there and open the place as the Society's headquarters and field station? He admitted that the house was almost a ruin but he emphasised on the other hand what a naturalists' paradise it was. There were owls in the roof, bats in the bedrooms, foxes on the ground floor and badgers in the cellars. He made no mention of who was going to make the house habitable for people or how we were supposed to get a living in so rural a spot. Inevitably this wild plan made no headway and soon afterwards the house was pulled down. Happily the estate is now cared for by the National Trust and there is even an ancient gold-mine where visitors are guided along chilly underground passages to learn how the Romans pursued the yellow metal deep into the hillside.

*   *   *

On July 27, 1946, an identity ring bearing the message: 'Zoological Museum, Copenhagen 272062' was put on the leg of a young white-fronted goose in the Christianhaab district of western Greenland. Six months later that ill-starred goose, one of a large flock, was shot on Tregaron Bog in Cardiganshire, the first ringed Greenland white-front to be found on the British mainland, though several had been recovered in Ireland. Over the years, as birdwatching increased in popularity, those Tregaron geese were to become quite famous, for they were the only Greenland white-fronts in all Wales. Year after year they were reliably there from October to April, sometimes as many as six hundred of them. Not that they kept all in one flock.

The River Teifi winding through Tregaron Bog National Nature Reserve.

Instead they were scattered in small groups all over the bog or the surrounding farmlands, so that wherever you went they rose with wild music and settled again not far away. They were an enjoyable background for all who braved a walk across the bog in winter.

It was on May 27, 1948, that I first got to Tregaron Bog. I went by train from Aberystwyth on that famous line that used to run (if that isn't too flattering a description of its progress) all the way to Carmarthen until 1963 when, after ninety-seven years of service, it was closed by bat-blind politicians. The trains, all steam in those days, used to puff heavily up from the coast to Strata Florida station and from there they cut across the eastern part of the bog and soon came to another stop at Allt Ddu Halt where there was usually no one to get on or off. Yet Allt Ddu Halt did serve a purpose: every summer it had at least one swallow's nest inside its doorless waiting room.

A moment in that first journey across the bog remains clear in my memory. Between Strata Florida and Allt Ddu the train passed right through the middle of a colony of black-headed gulls sitting calmly on their nests in a swamp colourful with bog beans all in pink and white flower. It was one of those sudden intimate glimpses of wildlife that travellers enjoy from rural railways the world over. Certainly the closest views I ever had of the Tregaron geese were from the train in winter when they were grazing nonchalantly a few yards from the line and didn't even look up as the train clattered by.

All the tales that are told everywhere about sleepy, rustic railways used to be recounted with relish about the Carmarthen to Aberystwyth line: how the driver would stop the train to pick mushrooms or collect his milk from a local farm; how trains were inadvertently shunted into sidings and forgotten for hours; how the engine one day ran out of coal, leaving the passengers to walk the last two miles into Aberystwyth. But a story that had a ring of truth about it concerned a couple of zoology students who caught an adder on Tregaron Bog and decided to take it back to the college laboratories at Aberystwyth to study it in captivity. On the train the adder escaped and was wandering about the compartment, much to the consternation of the passengers, there being no corridors on those trains. In all history there can have been no travellers more relieved to reach Aberystwyth than those who journeyed in that compartment that day from Tregaron.

On my first visit I stayed at Tregaron several days exploring the bog and the surrounding district with Jack Davies, an Aberystwyth geography student with a passion for the whole world of natural history. We soon discovered what a rare wilderness it was, this miry waste so improbably surviving undrained in a drainage-mad world, a fragment of ancient landscape with the Teifi river winding through it all. Peat-cutters had nibbled at its edges but only to feed local hearths. Otherwise its peat was intact and with it all the peat vegetation—the sheets of gleaming white cotton-grass; the wide domes of heather; the vast spreads of rushes and moorgrass; sundews of three kinds; bog rosemary, bog asphodel, bog mosses; white beak-sedge by the acre (and therefore large heath butterflies which feed on it); and a whole world of other plants for whom the sour soils of peat-bogs are the sweetest of all environments.

It was the birds that interested us most—the many yodelling curlews, the plangent lapwings, the snipe that yickered and bleated everywhere, the few pairs of redshank and dunlin with their beautiful courtship songs, the quacking mallard, the piping teal. From pool to pool we followed the Teifi through its flood plain and we met with no one in that lonely place. If either of us were in need of Thoreau's 'tonic of wildness' we found it in those few miles of peat, water, rush, moorgrass and heather which had so triumphantly defied the destructive centuries.

After that first visit I went there many times. In those early post-war days there was a fervour everywhere for the burgeoning idea of nature conservation; and when naturalists looked at mid-Wales, Tregaron Bog was put high on the list of proposed reserves, its uniqueness having been pointed out long before by field-workers of the calibre of John H. Salter, Bertram Lloyd and Charles Oldham. I was fourteen years too late to see one of the bog's former breeding birds. There are no records to tell us how long those lesser black-backed gulls had been there. J. H. Salter knew them in 1893. Seven years later he thought there were fifty pairs. At Tregaron on June 28, 1921, Bertram Lloyd wrote in his diary: 'Lesser black-backed gulls; over 100 yelling round my head when I passed their breeding territory'. A year later he estimated their number as at least 150 and also noted a few herring gulls among them. But another twelve months brought their population down to a mere thirty birds. Game-keepers had declared war on them and the end was in sight. Frank Best recorded a few pairs nesting there in June 1934, and they were the last. Their passing was a sad loss. I know that lesser black-backed gulls are not everybody's favourites but that inland-breeding Tregaron population was, like the cormorants on Craig yr Aderyn, something rare in Wales and fully deserving protection.

I soon learnt that even in summer Tregaron Bog is not always idyllic. On a hot July day the horse-flies can be unbearable. And I shall not forget the night I ventured to sleep on the banks of the Teifi in mid-bog in the hope of seeing otters at dawn: long before midnight I was driven away by mosquitos. Summer rains, too, can be quite phenomenal, as they were for the visit of the British Ecological Society on July 23, 1954. That morning, as I left home, our little Einion river at Eglwys-fach was a brown and boiling Amazon, filling the valley with its rage and thunder; and down in the village I heard that the Royal Welsh Show in Machynlleth was knee-deep in water. By the time I reached Tregaron the rain was as heavy as ever and so it continued all day. Not that our Welsh weather daunted the eminent English ecologists present, including Professor A. R. Clapham of Clapham, Tutin and Warburg's *Flora of the British Isles* which had appeared two years earlier. Our leader, Hugh Chater, had planned a route for us across the bog which necessitated getting over the river on a long tree trunk which had a precarious railing attached to it. There would have been no problem on a fine day with the Teifi a friendly murmuring stream. But in a gale of rain, with the river nearly up to bridge level, the crossing really was hazardous and Hugh Chater stationed several of us downstream to rescue anyone who might slip into the flood. Amazingly we all crossed safely and, despite the weather, everyone managed to see most of the plants and learn something about the ecological history of this bog that began as a lake at the end of the Ice Age and was nearly a lake again on the day of our visit. Today this ancient peatbog is a highly valued National Nature Reserve. Its popular Welsh name is Cors Caron but on many older maps it was the more descriptive Cors Goch Glan Teifi ('the

Red Bog along the Teifi'), which tells of the rich colour of the stems of cotton-grass, rushes and other plants especially when sunshine lights up the scene late in a winter afternoon.

*　　*　　*

For many miles the coast north of the Dyfi estuary must be a great disappointment to cliff-nesting seabirds. Long stretches have no cliffs at all, and where any cliffs exist they are often small and crumbling. But the cormorants got over this problem long ago. Maybe back in the days of prehistory, they began to breed on Craig yr Aderyn (Bird Rock), a towering crag four miles inland near Tywyn, and there they remain, about forty-five pairs of them. I first went there in 1950 to investigate, for the West Wales Field Society, a report that the nesting cormorants were being used as target practice by rifle shooters. In those days there was little sympathy for cormorants. In fact, a local angling association was offering ten shillings each for the heads of both cormorants and otters. The Field Society was fortunate in its quest: the owner of Craig yr Aderyn was happy for us to put up a notice saying that the rock was now a nature reserve and the birds have gone undisturbed ever since.

Some days you may see cormorants roosting on Craig yr Aderyn even in autumn and winter, along with choughs and a whole crowd of jackdaws. When I got there one grey November afternoon I could see cormorants coming in one after another up the valley from the sea. It was too dark to count how many were already on the ledges but those arriving were still clear enough as black shapes cut out against the sky. Many came in high up and passed over the summit to circle back, planing down at speed on rigid wings, then braking sharply just before alighting on the cliff. One or two circled up really high as if simply for the thrill of plunging headlong to their roosts, their wings half-closed. From nearly a thousand feet below I could hear the tearing sound of the air through their feathers. As each bird landed it was greeted by grunts and growls from those already on the ledges. Then it was deep dusk and the cormorants' day was over.

A botanical mystery lies in wait for you at Craig yr Aderyn. In the late seventeenth century Edward Lhuyd, who first reported the cormorants there, also mentioned that mountain everlasting (*Antennaria dioica*) grew 'on a mountain called Cefn Llwyd, ye back side of Craig yr Aderyn. . . in flower plentifully'. It doesn't seem to be there now, so when did it die out and why? This is far from being the only locality from which the plant has vanished. It is apparently persisting quite well in limestone habitats but has gone from many limeless places like the Craig yr Aderyn area. Can we assume that acid rain has so tipped the balance against it in sour-soiled districts that it can now survive only amid the sweetness of limestone? It is a grievous loss for this is one of our most attractive and interesting wild plants with its two-coloured flowers, the males usually white, the females pink.

⋆   ⋆   ⋆

On a Saturday morning in April, 1951, Ronald Lockley picked me up in Eglwys-fach and together we went to the Caernarfonshire village of Chwilog near Pwllheli. There, on a beautiful estate, with house and lake to match, lived Rupert Williams-Ellis and his wife, Cecily. The occasion was a meeting they had convened to look into, amongst other matters, the possibility of setting up a bird observatory on Ynys Enlli (Bardsey Island) as Lockley had done years before on Skokholm.

One result of that meeting was that Penny and I camped on Bardsey for a week in August, 1952, and were completely captivated by its charm. So people have probably always felt about this very livable island. Certainly in the Middle Ages its abbey of St Mary was enormously popular as a place of pilgrimage. To be buried on such a holy island was even better: it meant you were pretty well guaranteed a place in Heaven. A discovery we made on that first visit was that for years the eggs of choughs, peregrines, ravens and seabirds had gone to a dealer on the mainland. So our first act, as soon as we were off the island, was to phone Cecily Williams-Ellis to advise her of the urgent need to prevent further egg-collecting. We were also able to tell her that there was an empty house on the island which would make an ideal bird observatory.

By chance, a few months before we got to Bardsey, Tony Norris of the West Midlands Bird Club had stayed there and had also seen its

86

Cormorants, part of a colony of c.45 pairs, nesting on Craig yr Aderyn near Tywyn, Meirionnydd.

Purple saxifrage (with icicles) on Cader Idris in March.

Yellow whitlow-grass is found in the British Isles only on the cliffs of Gower.

possibilities as a bird-watching station. So on behalf of the West Wales Field Society I got in touch with Tony and after various discussions with him and his fellow West Midlands stalwart, Cecil Lambourne, we decided to go ahead with the observatory idea in collaboration with Cecily Williams-Ellis and her north Wales friends. A sadness was that Rupert Williams-Ellis had died without seeing the fulfilment of his dream of a wildlife centre on Bardsey. The observatory was opened in 1953 and flourishes to this day. People stay there at little expense and they enjoy the experience of island life, the seabirds, the birds of passage, the playful choughs, the singing seals and the wild flowers (blue sheets of vernal squills in the spring). The sea winds often blow and the waves are ever bursting up the rocks. It is all very exhilarating and enjoyable as long as you are happy to accept the possibility of delayed boat-crossings and the certainty of living conditions not all that different from those of the medieval monks.

'Shearwatering' is a popular Bardsey pursuit. It is for dark nights only because shearwaters, fearful of predatory hawks and gulls, have learnt never to come to land by daylight or even by moonlight. On a still, warm evening we take the steep path up through the gorse to the top of Mynydd Enlli (Bardsey Mountain). There we sit and wait. We watch the summer twilight deepen and the mainland, two miles away, slowly fade until it becomes a long shadow floating on the sea. Then it vanishes. All is now dark about us and there is silence except for the far-off murmur of the tide in Bardsey Sound.

Faint and high overhead a strangled crowing. It dies away but returns, louder. It is joined by others until the air is full of wild shrieks, sobbings and wailings. Not dozens but hundreds of shearwaters have arrived for their nightly visit from the sea. We listen to their wings rustling in the darkness and soon we hear bird after bird thumping onto the turf all round us, sometimes at our feet. We switch on a torch. Now we can see them, quite sizeable black and white birds scuttling into burrows or just crouching on the ground. We easily pick them up, for on such a windless night they are unable to take flight unless they have a rock, a mound or a slope from which to launch themselves. For a few seconds I hold one in my hands and in the torchlight I see its soft dark eyes looking into mine. It tries to

Manx shearwater photographed by flash at midnight on the top of Bardsey Mountain.

scratch me with the sharp claws on its webbed feet. Then its long thin beak comes round and nips my wrists, fetching blood. When I pùt it down it scrambles across the turf and up a bank. From there it flutters forwards, finds its wings and is gone into the night. I waste a lot of film trying to photograph the shearwaters in flight. No matter, it is wonderful to stand there high above the sea under the wide starry sky and have this multitude of birds flying so close and occasionally colliding with me. It is exciting too when I press the shutter and see these long-winged fowls of the ocean revealed in brilliant detail by the flash. And if I forget all else I shall remember their thousand voices caterwauling through the blackness of a summer night.

'Shearwatering' has a serious purpose. Though shearwaters have been much studied, a great deal remains to be found out about them. On Bardsey, as at other large colonies, as many as possible are ringed, weighed and measured, and gradually the details of their life-history are being pieced together. Who would have thought, in pre-ringing days, that many, perhaps most, of our shearwaters spend the winter off the coast of Argentina? Or that in a lifetime of thirty years they may return to nest, spring after spring, in the same burrow as before? Once, a shearwater ringed on Skokholm was found in Australia. So who knows what marvels still await discovery about these mysterious ocean travellers?

Under the chaos of fallen boulders at the bottom of Bardsey's steep eastern slopes there is hidden a sea-cave much frequented by seals. If you are reasonably slim and agile you can crawl down into the back of this dusky cavern and from a rocky ledge get an exciting view of what goes on in the water as if you are sitting in a theatre. One day as we looked down into six feet of green water, a pallid shape came gliding in through the sunlit cave entrance and surfaced just below us. It was a female seal about five feet in length. For a moment or two she swam round on the surface and then, looking up, she noticed us,

A female seal photographed by flash in Seal Cave, Bardsey Island.

two ghostly faces staring silently down at her. Her reaction was typically seal-like. She stared back at us, her large expressive eyes full of what seemed like puzzlement. Then she dived quite silently, her lithe body curving with a delicious movement out through the cave exit and she was gone. A few minutes later she was back, again surfacing just below us and again staring at us silently, inquisitively. For an hour we sat there while this graceful white seal came and stared and went, then came and stared and went many times, never showing fear, only intense interest, trying to understand what we

Summer tanager, Bardsey Island, September 1957, the only record of this American bird in Europe.

R. S. Thomas bird-watching on Bardsey Island, October 1971.

were, two indistinct shapes of creatures she perhaps saw too dimly to recognise as human. It was one of the strangest experiences I have known with a wild animal, this looking into a seal's inquiring eyes in the green shadows of that cave. Watching her it was easy to see how the idea of mermaids first came swimming into men's thoughts.

A final Bardsey cameo. I am sitting on a rock above the sea watching a pair of choughs bringing nest material off the beach and disappearing with it into a cave where they breed every year. The sky is azure, the air has a rare stillness, there is a scent of gorse in bloom. After a while the choughs must feel the perfection of the hour, for they take a rest from their nest-making and begin to circle above me. Up and up they go, round and round on rigid wings, like a pair of buzzards, effortlessly. As they rise they find the lightest of breezes that drifts them slowly out over the sea. Still rising they eventually pass even beyond the range of my binoculars. I try to visualise how the island must look to them from so high in the heavens. Time passes and my attention turns to rock pipits, wheatears, oyster-catchers, kittiwakes and far-away plunging gannets. I don't notice the choughs' return but suddenly here they are just over my head again, frolicking in the air and calling cheerful messages to each other. I am cross with myself for missing what may have been a spectacular earthward plunge.

The most optimistic field meeting I ever organised was to take a group of the West Wales Field Society from Dolgellau to the end of the north Wales peninsula to visit the gull islands which lie a mile off Aberdaron and four miles north-east of Bardsey. These twin islets, Ynys Gwylan Fawr and Ynys Gwylan Fach, are part of a mostly submerged reef of the igneous rock called dolerite and are impossible to land on except in the calmest weather. We went by road to Aberdaron and then took to the sea in an open motor boat. Having got landing permission from the islands' owner, we had arranged many weeks before for this boat to pick us up off the beach at Aberdaron, land us on Gwylan Fawr and take us back later.

Anyone who knows that Land's End of north Wales and how the seas can sometimes rage round it for weeks on end, will appreciate that the number of days in a year that a boat can take passengers off Aberdaron beach are rather few. And that there is even less likelihood of landing people safely on the slippery, seaweedy rocks of Ynys Gwylan Fawr. Yet on June 12, 1954, as if ordained by Neptune himself, the sea was so still that a halcyon might quite safely have built herself a floating nest off Aberdaron, and we moved gently over to Gwylan Fawr on the smoothest of waters. My most treasured memory of the crossing was of one of the ladies, Miss Dorothy Davies, a teacher at Dolgellau's Dr Williams School, who wore with the greatest elegance a wide-brimmed summer hat which floated from her head half-way across. The boatman got a cheer as, having swung the boat round, he managed to retrieve this valuable property.

Gwylan Fawr, we discovered, was wholly given over to seabirds and to plants that love the sea winds. The star performers were the ever delightful puffins that whirred around our heads and popped in and out of burrows a few yards from us. We felt as if we were landing on some island of the Galapagos. There were also gulls, guillemots, razorbills, shags and oystercatchers nesting everywhere and all were remarkably unafraid of us. The plants were largely a mat of scurvy-grass, orache, thrift, rock spurrey and those amazing tree mallows that hold themselves so erect in all the gales that blow. Never since that day have I thought of arranging another trip to Ynys Gwylan Fawr. There must after all be a limit to the amount of magic even Neptune has at his disposal.

★   ★   ★

Turning the pages of my old diaries I have sometimes wondered why I've gone to the trouble of writing them; but I suppose a devoted diarist, however unconsciously, must be at heart a compulsive archivist, to whom the summing up of each day comes as naturally as having supper. Since my late teens I have kept diaries with few gaps except for those lost years of the Second World War. They have never been personal diaries in the Samuel Pepys sense of the word. My chronicles are not at all concerned with the daily happenings of life, no matter how momentous, unless they are linked with natural history. So on many days, especially in winter, I have had nothing to report except the weather. Yet even those brief notes on the wind, the rain and the temperature are a thread on which to string my days together. And sometimes I have found it useful to be able to look back and discover how hot was the sun or how deep the snow on such and such a date. All I know for sure is that I treasure my old diaries and enjoy turning back their pages to recover so much that would otherwise now be lost without trace.

When I think of nature diaries I think of Gilbert White. All of us love his *Selborne* for the masterpiece it is. Yet we should not neglect his diaries, so effective with their short, laconic, largely uncompleted sentences so refreshingly short on adjectives, so delightfully using the present tense. Witness his entry for January 21, 1793: 'Thrush sings, the song thrush: the missle thrush has not been heard. On this day Louis 16th, late King of France, was beheaded at Paris'. (Note the correct order of priority he gives to these events.) So he goes on all his life like a calmly flowing river. Here he is in 1779:

> Aug. 21. Sun, brisk air, sweet even. Many people have finished wheat harvest.
> Aug. 27. Full moon. My well is shallow and the water foul.
> Aug. 29. House crickets are heard in all the gardens and court-yards. One came to my kitchen hearth.

93

Aug. 31. The grass burns.

Sept. 2. Partridges innumerable. Barley harvest finished here.

Sept. 6. The trufle-hunter trie's my brother's groves; but finds few trufles and those very small. They want moisture.

Reading White's tranquil record it is hard not to be envious of what must have been a wonderful age for a naturalist to have lived in, a time when there was so little threat to the countryside compared with our destructive century which has diverted so many naturalists away from natural history into desperate, often hopeless, conservation struggles. Perhaps never in his life did it occur to White that life around Selborne would ever alter very much. True, he notes that in his day the blackcock and the deer had gone from Wolmer Forest but on the whole he has few changes to report or anticipate.

Contrast White's world with that of another nature-diarist, Henry D. Thoreau of Massachusetts. Thoreau was just as possessed by natural history as White had been. Yet though he was born only twenty-four years after White died, the world had already lurched heavily in the direction of industrialisation. As he lived those crucial two years in his cabin by Walden Pond, Thoreau was acutely aware of the railway recently built nearby and he knew that its clanking engines were a symbol of huge changes that would soon be hurtling society in a direction in which he, for one, had no desire to go. So Thoreau's journals are tinged with an unease we do not find in White.

In the early 1950s I was more concerned with Thoreau than with Gilbert White. Ronald Lockley was editing a series of biographies of great naturalists. For himself he had chosen Gilbert White and he invited me to write a life of Thoreau because he knew I was a Thoreau enthusiast. So in 1953 I immersed myself in things Thoreauvian and my little book appeared the following year. I enjoyed getting involved with a subject so dear to my heart; and as it was my first book I began to learn a little about the strange world of writing and publishing.

Chapter 6

Although over the years I have written much about wildflowers and trees and have spent countless happy botanical days in the field, I am far from being a botanist. A plant-seeker, yes. A botanist, no, I am too short on science for that. But 'plant-seeker' has an awkward ring about it and I'm sorry the language has dropped the old word 'simpler', meaning a seeker of simples or herbs. 'A simple simpler' would describe me perfectly.

It was in 1949 that Penny and I began to take a serious interest in wildflowers. In the spring of that year we bought Bentham and Hooker's *Handbook of the British Flora*, a popular work then in its seventh edition. George Bentham was a high-powered botanist for whom writing the *British Flora* had merely been a 'before-breakfast relaxation' intended 'for the use of beginners and amateurs'. First published as long ago as 1858, Bentham and Hooker's *Handbook* was not to be superseded till 1952 when, to keep up to date, everyone had to go out and buy *The Flora of the British Isles* by Clapham, Tutin and Warburg.

In the 1950s we had the good fortune to have many days out with three first-rate botanists, all now long gone a-simpling in the Elysian Fields. I have already mentioned Hugh Chater, a lecturer in ecology at Aberystwyth. It chanced that he and his wife, Peggy, had a holiday cottage near Ponterwyd when we were living there. Right from the start they were extremely kind to us and they got us ever more interested in the flora of upland Cardiganshire, showing us grasses, sedges, clubmosses, sundews and other treasures which till then we had tended to pass by almost un-noticed and certainly un-named. From that time onwards for nearly thirty years Hugh and Peggy Chater were to help us not only in botany but in countless other ways.

Into our lives in 1953 came another friend who was to lead us even further into the realm of green plants. Mary Richards of Dolgellau was a lady whose enthusiasm was prodigious and infectious. Ty'nllidiart, her cottage that looked across to the great cliffs of Cader

Idris four miles away, was an open house for botanists from all over the country, especially from Kew Herbarium where she had several friends. She loved to take her visitors up Cader to show them the alpine plants, and even in her old age most of them got tired before she did. Going out so often with Mary Richards we learnt much about the flora of the botanically rich country around Dolgellau. And about birds, mammals, insects and everything else.

Evidently anxious to make sure that Penny and I would for ever hold the world of plants in a warm embrace, the fates introduced us to yet another inspiring botanist. Price Evans, son of a quarryman from Corris, had had a distinguished teaching career in the north of England and was now living in retirement at Degannwy near Llandudno. Though a keen botanist, Price Evans preferred to be known as that then modern phenomenon, an ecologist. In 1914 he had been one of the founders, with Arthur Tansley, of the British Ecological Society, and it was he who spurred on Mary Richards to found (March 21, 1953) the Merioneth section of the West Wales Field Society, now a branch of the North Wales Wildlife Trust. If ever a man was possessed by a mountain that man was Price Evans. For forty years he devoted every summer holiday to studying the rocks, soils and plants of Cader Idris about which he wrote two pioneering papers in the *Journal of Ecology* (1932 and 1945). In his retirement he was in demand as a leader of field meetings, shepherding us forth in sunshine or in rain, lecturing us in the sweetest way in the world about why plants grow here but not there, or there but not here. Both Hugh Chater and Price Evans, as ecologists, taught us and so many others not only to look at plants but also to think about them and their place in the world.

Guided by Price Evans we began to grasp something of the ecology of Cader Idris and why some cliffs were curtained with green vegetation while others were gaunt and naked precipices with not a leaf of any plant in sight. We ventured along slippery ledges farther than was really safe; peered into caves for rare ferns; slithered, almost tobogganed, down endless screes; sloshed across marshes and waded into lakes in search of water plants. Price Evans enjoyed recounting how one day, while botanising on Cader Idris, he came upon a geologist who explained that he was trying to trace a certain band of

The Cader Idris range from the A470 east of Cross Foxes.

igneous rock across the mountain's north face. To this geologist's total amazement Price Evans felt in his pocket and brought out a map with the said band of rock clearly marked on it for several miles. He then had to show this laborious tapper of the rocks how the outcrop he was seeking was child's play for a botanist to follow because it was rich enough in lime to attract lime-loving plants that are quite absent from the rest of this acid-soiled mountain. All that was needed was the ability to identify the little fern called green spleenwort and one or two calcicole mosses; or a few alpine wildflowers such as purple saxifrage, mossy saxifrage, lesser meadow-rue or mountain sorrel. For the record, the geologist in the story was Arthur Hubert Cox who was to become the author of a classic paper on the geology of Cader Idris in 1925.

Hugh Chater used to tell a story to illustrate Price Evans's devotion to his favourite mountain. He happened to bump into Price Evans in a London street (they were both heading for a Nature Conservancy meeting). 'Having exchanged greetings', said Chater, 'it took Price Evans just two minutes to get on to the subject of the Upper Basic rocks of Cader Idris while London's traffic roared all round us.'

If Price Evans had a favourite Cader Idris plant it was *Genista pilosa*, a dwarf shrub with yellow pea flowers. In English it is hairy greenweed though there can be nothing at all weedy about a plant which has probably faced Cader's weather for a vast reach of time. Curiously rare in Britain it has had a patchy history on Cader Idris, its only British mountain locality. It was found up there before 1800 but was then lost sight of so completely that it was dismissed in the nineteenth century as an error. It was not refound until 1901 and then seems to have been lost again till Price Evans came upon it in 1927. Since then botanists have kept a regular eye on *Genista pilosa* and have now shown it to be more widespread on the Cader range than had been thought. For two reasons it is an elusive plant: when not in bloom it is far from eye-catching, and when its flowers do appear they are very soon over. Strangely, though it steadfastly faces awesome frosts not only on Cader but also on the Continent, it is best known in Britain on the coasts of Pembrokeshire and Cornwall where you might well suppose it to be a tenderling in need of a frost-free seaside climate.

In July 1956, the chance came for Penny and me to go and see the real alpine world. In a little van we drove through Belgium, France and Germany, camping along the way. So we came to Switzerland's Engadine and climbed through the zone of natural pine forest up into a world of gleaming limestone crags where there were flowers in delirious abundance: primulas, saxifrages, androsaces, drabas, silenes, ericas, saponarias, gentians and a huge number of others. Some were but tiny flecks of colour, others were bright cushions we could see from far away. Most had their roots wedged tight in crevices; others, like the little purple soldanellas, peeped shyly out of the melting snow. We even found edelweiss though it had become quite rare through over-collecting. We saw birds that were new: honey buzzard, nutcracker, alpine swift, serin, woodchat shrike,

Bonelli's warbler; and above the forests, alpine accentor, water pipit and citril finch.

After a fortnight in the company of the wonderful alpine flora (not to mention the huge wealth of sub-alpine plants) we came back to Wales, to Cwm Einion. As we zigzagged up our little hillside track we thought of the super-zigzags of Switzerland climbing for thousands of feet. The purple bell-heather along our road was now at its brightest. So was the deep-yellow of the autumn gorse. At the top of the climb we looked back at the estuary where the flood tide was a dark-red ribbon in the setting sun. We had seen the Jungfrau shining in the sunlight; the Rhone glacier by moonlight; Lake Lucerne mirror-smooth below Mount Pilatus; and from the highest ridges of the Jura we had looked across to Mont Blanc and the whole snowy skyline of the Alps. Yet none was lovelier than the sun sinking into the hills beyond the Dyfi estuary; and the wide heavens stretching in broad yellow and black bands over the sea towards Ireland. And already a nightjar was beginning to chur from somewhere amongst the rocks and bracken of Foel Fawr.

★   ★   ★

Harlech Castle, high above the shores of Meirionnydd, has always been my favourite medieval relic. Perhaps this is because it caught me young. I was five when I was first taken to see it but my infant memory is not so much of ancient walls and soaring towers but of jackdaws, millions (as it seemed to me) of chackety-chacking jackdaws swirling in the air or crowded along the parapets. I watched this multitude with total astonishment because back home in Harborne we seldom saw a jackdaw from one year's end to the other. I was fascinated to learn that when Harlech Castle was built in the thirteenth century it stood excitingly on the brink of a sea-cliff. I pictured wild waves crashing and spuming up the rocks under the castle and felt cheated that this no longer happens and that a wide tract of land now lies between the castle and the sea. But what I did not know then was that the sand-dunes (called Morfa Harlech) which were created by the gales of the late Middle Ages, are so wonderfully rich in wildlife.

Looking north over the dunes of Morfa Harlech National Nature Reserve.
Highest of the distant hills (centre right) is Moel Hebog.

It was thirty years later that Penny and I got to know Morfa
Harlech and its beautiful dune flora—the fragrant mats of rest-
harrow, lady's bedstraw and wild thyme along with hound's tongue,
blue fleabane, maiden pink, burnet rose, quaking grass, fairy flax,
pyramidal orchids and a bewildering multitude of marsh orchids,
many of them hybrids of marvellous stature. There were also
countless marsh helleborines growing in all the damp hollows
amongst forests of creeping willow. One summer those knee-high
willows were crawling with almost a plague of poplar hawkmoth
caterpillars. Yet such are the ups and downs of insect life that we
couldn't find any at all the following summer. In those early visits to
Morfa Harlech, as to so many other choice localities, our botanical
guides were usually Mary Richards and Peter Benoit. Who better
than these two enthusiasts who were then working on their list of
Merioneth plants which appeared in 1961?

One June night I slept, or rather tried to sleep, near the willow-girt pool in the heart of those Morfa Harlech dunes. Too late I discovered that the hundred or so pairs of black-headed gulls that nested round the pool not only called, yelled and shrieked all day but also most of the night as well. I was glad when dawn came and I could go for a walk round the *morfa* and along the nearby estuary. On my way back I had just reached the crest of one of the highest dunes when I had the dream-like experience of seeing a pair of Montagu's harriers, the male almost white, the female dark-brown, floating lightly past. I suppose they had a nest somewhere near, for in the fifties it was not nearly such a rare event to see Montagu's harriers here as it would be today. Until the early 1960s there were breeding pairs scattered from Newborough in Anglesey to St David's in Pembrokeshire. Then all vanished.

Exploring Meirionnydd with Mary Richards, Peter Benoit and others,' we got to know upland meadows here and there where we could still find many plants which had already long gone from most lowland fields in the cause of grassland improvement: globe flower, yellow rattle, upright vetch, petty whin, marsh hawksbeard, wood horsetail, various sedges, moonwort, adders-tongue, not to mention marsh orchids, spotted orchids, butterfly orchids, fragrant orchid, frog orchid and even the rare small white orchid. Then came years when we watched in sadness as these high-level meadows were ploughed, re-seeded and artificially fertilised in the name of progress. There was no use blaming the farmers for this vandalism. They had little choice but to carry out the policies of the Ministry of Agriculture.

In 1953 we first got into the heart of a range of hills we had often looked at from afar. They were what we then called the Rhinogs but which, with a better acquaintance with the language of Heaven, we learned to call the Rhinogydd. Stretching for over fourteen miles between Maentwrog and Barmouth, these Rhinogydd are beautifully seen from the main road as you move north from Dolgellau to Trawsfynydd. Deep in trees, mostly conifers, you pass up the valley from Ganllwyd, then suddenly you come clear of all leafy or needly canopy and away on your left is this startling mountainy outline cut out clean and black, if it is late afternoon, against the western sky.

Our first walk across the Rhinogydd was not from there but from the west. We came, as many do, up the winding valley of the Artro with its ancient, moss-grown oakwoods. Our guide was Randolph Stringer who lived in a charmingly sequestered woodland house within sound of the river. One of his passions was butterflies and he had even tried to introduce swallowtails and their food-plant from Norfolk to his garden here in Wales! Locally his speciality was the now declining marsh fritillary of which he had discovered several colonies on the Rhinog boglands.

On a mild day in mid-November we skirted the deep, dark waters of Llyn Cwm Bychan and saw intimately before us the cliffs and terraces of naked stone which make this north end of Rhinog one of the most barren uplands in all Snowdonia. Above the lake a path climbed alongside a tree-shaded, chattering stream and soon, all woodland behind us, we came to where the track changed from beaten earth to a carefully paved way. We had reached the most remarkable road in Wales, the so-called Roman Steps. As we made our way up the steps we tried to count them but soon gave up when we realised they ran into thousands as they curved out of sight up through the scree and the tumbled boulders, sometimes dividing into two paths and in one place even into three.

Expertly gradiented these steps were only possible because the rock here, a hard grit of Cambrian age, splits so readily into suitable slabs. They were presumably built with such labour not in Roman times but in the Middle Ages when there was a need to have a trackway from Harlech Castle to Bala (which had political links with Harlech) and so on into England. We lunched in deep heather overlooking the little rock-girt lake called Llyn Morwynion. Despite the quiet, warm November sunshine, not a bird nor an insect stirred. At that season the uplands are already deep into thoughts about winter.

It was not till the following summer (June 1954) that we took our next walk up the Roman Steps. This time we had distinguished botanical company: Mary Richards, busy on her flora of the county; and her friend, Edgar Milne-Redhead of Kew Herbarium, who was here on holiday. But fog came low and without the steps to guide us we would soon have been lost. We thought how the travellers of many centuries must often have been grateful for this staircase through the uplands; for fogs are many on these sea-facing flanks of Rhinog. The Roman Steps are edged by so much heather and bilberry that there is little hope of finding much else, especially in a fog. But on our way back to the lakeside at Cwm Bychan, where the visibility was better, we managed to find three good plants: the intermediate sundew, which is so tiny, and two ferns of contrasting dimensions—the minute moonwort and the huge and stately royal fern.

We were up there again a few weeks later because at that time the Nature Conservancy was trying to decide whether or where to set up a Rhinog National Nature Reserve and had sought the help of Mary Richards and other amateur botanists. So we walked, stumbled and staggered across the whole range from Foel Ysgyfarnogod in the north—a challenging wilderness of fissured rocks and waist-deep heather—south to the craggy heights of Rhinog Fawr and Rhinog Fach and the grassier domes of Y Llethr and Diffwys. We found lakes and hidden lakelets with quillwort, shoreweed and lobelia, as well as pondweeds, water lilies and other plants that float. Deep cracks in the rocks were upholstered with mosses and lichens. We floundered through bogs rich in sundews and sedges. Parting the heather we saw many pale-purple spikes of the lesser twayblade, one of the smallest of British orchids. We saw a herd of those vari-coloured, shaggy-haired, hugely horned goats-gone-wild which have long lived a life of their own in these high solitudes. We heard the barking of distant grouse of which only a few now remained of the multitudes Mary Richards remembered from her childhood days of over half a century before.

You can't wander far over these wild hills without realising that this is a district rich in the traces of those who lived and (more obviously) died in the days of prehistory. Not that I have ever had any itch to take up archaeology. I could never imagine myself digging and sifting patiently through ancient living floors or burial places in the hope of shedding light on the life-styles of vanished generations, only to reveal that they were no more edifying than those of today. All the same I am happy to think that their relics have endured so long: the Neolithic chambered tombs of Carneddau Hengwm near Barmouth and those at Dyffryn; the scatter of fine upright stones of the Bronze

Age which has also bequeathed to us the remote and beautiful little circle on Bryn Cader Faner; and the several hill forts and village remains of the Iron Age. More than anything on Rhinog I have enjoyed the ancient trackways though sometimes they have lost themselves (and me) miles from anywhere.

*   *   *

One day when John Davies ('John-y-post'), then the birdwatcher-postman of Aberdyfi, told me he had just found a great spotted cuckoo lying dead under some trees, I was not sure, as the date was April 1st, whether he was pulling my leg or not. But when he handed me the bird later there was no doubt about it. It was clearly a cuckoo but obviously not a common cuckoo: it was boldly pale-spotted and much bigger and darker than the cuckoos we are used to. Its tail was heavily blotched with white and, most strikingly, it had a prominent white head crest. How I wished it had been alive so that we could have seen it in action and heard its harsh, chattering voice. For that we would have to go to Spain which is no doubt where this bird had wanted to get to. As it migrated up the west coast of Africa it must have got blown so far out into the Atlantic by off-shore winds that it didn't make land until it reached the Welsh coast in a state of exhaustion. It was extremely thin and had obviously died of hunger. Such was the unhappy fate of the first great spotted cuckoo recorded for Wales, the sixth for the British Isles.

1957 was a memorable year for our local birders. On June 25 I heard on the phone that a strange duck was nesting near Aberdyfi on an islet in the estuary that is part of the grounds of the house called Trefri. I went to investigate and was just in time to see the nest full of newly hatched ducklings before they made for the water. They were hidden under rhododendrons behind a garden seat, and I wondered how many people had sat on that seat in the previous four weeks never suspecting that there was a very nervous duck on her eggs four feet away. As I approached the spot the duck fluttered off down the rocks into the water and I saw that she was a red-breasted merganser, a bird which had never before nested so far south in Wales.

104

The fifties were an expanding time for mergansers. Before that, though regularly seen on the Dyfi and other Welsh estuaries in winter, they had been restricted as a breeding species mainly to Scotland and Ireland. Then in 1953 a pair nested in Wales (on the north coast of Anglesey) and from then on there was a steady advance south until four years later here they were nesting on the northern bank of the Dyfi. Next year a pair crossed the estuary to breed under the heronry at Ynys-hir, thus reaching south Wales. Since then mergansers have spread widely in Wales and have been followed by another northern diving duck, the goosander. Our birders have been delighted; our anglers less so, for mergansers and goosanders, with their long, saw-like bills, are highly efficient catchers of fish.

*   *   *

In July 1957, the Montgomeryshire Field Society and the Merioneth branch of the West Wales Field Society held one of their occasional joint meetings. Very nearly a fiasco, it took place on one of those days of thick mist and rain when all moorland frolics ought to be called off. Yet this one was not. We met at Pistyll Rhaeadr, the high and graceful waterfall at Llanrhaeadr-ym-Mochnant, our intention being to climb Moel Sych, the loftiest point along the Berwyn moorlands. Recklessly we set off into the fog and only by a miracle did no one get lost, slip into a ravine or disappear into a bog-hole.

This was no ordinary weekend ramble but a botanical pilgrimage to look for the white-flowered, orange-fruited, thornless bramble called cloudberry which in Wales grows only on the heights of Berwyn. But to talk about the orange fruits of the Berwyn cloudberry may be misleading, for in some years it is reluctant to produce any. It is a plant that properly belongs to the arctic and the sub-arctic. It is locally common on the moors of Scotland and northern England. On Berwyn it is restricted to a zone at about two thousand feet. Why? And how, unarmed by any prickles, has it managed to survive up there amongst those all-devouring sheep?

Our expedition was a success in the sense that two or three of us managed to grope our way far enough up Moel Sych to be able to pick a few leaves of cloudberry to bring back for the rest to see. And everyone agreed that the weather was certainly just right for a plant with a name like cloudberry. But our leader wasn't having that. Cloudberry, he explained, has nothing to do with clouds. It came from an Old English word *clud* meaning a hill. Three centuries ago the Welsh botanist, Edward Lhuyd, was on the trail of cloudberry. Wishing to grow it at the Ashmolean Museum, Oxford, he sent for some Berwyn specimens, adding an instruction to the collector: 'Pray trace ye roots as far as you can; for soe much likelier they'l be to grow'. I wonder what success he had at Oxford with what he called these 'mwyar Berwyn' (Berwyn berries)?

The most thundery day I remember in Wales was the bank holiday Monday of August 5, 1957. All afternoon and evening the sky was black, the lightning spectacular and the rain almost tropical. The rivers rose in their wrath, angriest of all being the Ystwyth which flows into the sea at Aberystwyth. Its water was highest just before midnight and many trees and several bridges were brought down. In the path of the flood was our friends the Cadmans' house, Felin Abermâd, which by morning stood a yard deep in water; and when Arthur Cadman whistled his labrador, the dog came swimming in through the window. But though the dog was safe, Arthur's wildfowl collection was not. In the next few days, after the waters had receded, the geese picked up poisonous metal fragments washed downstream from old mine tips and there were casualties. It was a reminder of how vulnerable are so many streams and rivers in this region of countless disused lead, zinc and copper mines.

*   *   *

Reading J. H. Salter's flora of Cardiganshire we soon realised that there were many plants in the coastal region of the south that were rare or absent where we lived at the northern edge of the county. So one day we went south to New Quay and walked up to the headland. There the cliff flowers were all familiar to us but at the first beach south we were delighted to find the pinkish-white flowers of wood vetch, a strange plant to see on the shore because normally this rather uncommon vetch is resolutely an inlander, growing in coppices and hedgerows. Returning to New Quay we wandered through woodlands just outside the town and were struck by the luxuriance of hart's-tongue ferns, broad-leaved helleborines and black bryony; and there were wood spotted orchids of a stature we had never before dreamed of. So we had our first lesson in the influence of lime-rich boulder clay. Looking up the subject later we found that along this part of the coast the ice-sheets which moved south down the frozen Irish Sea brought with them huge quantities of fertile soil which, at the end of the Ice Age, they left deposited far and wide. But somehow north Cardiganshire was left out of these bonanzas and some of its farmers and gardeners have been battling with sour soils ever since.

After that first visit I have often been back to southern Cardiganshire and seen other lime-loving plants, notable early purple orchids in wondrous variety of size and colour; great mats of moschatel; dog's-mercury in sheets; soft shieldfern filling an entire valley; jungles of wild privet, giant horsetail and wild madder—all plants that are not so easy to find only a few miles north, such is the dichotomy of Cardiganshire. One day, picnicking on the little clay cliffs at Cei Bach, Penny and I were in a world of primroses and cowslips. Then we found one that struck us as odd until we realised that we had met with our first false oxlip, the primrose-cowslip hybrid. It had cowslip-like clusters of flowers that were half the size of primroses but twice as large as cowslip flowers and much paler.

1957 was the year I joined the *Manchester Guardian*'s (since 1961 the *Guardian*'s) team of country diarists. On October 9 I wrote my first diary: it was about butterflies in Indian summer weather; and I have gone babbling on ever since about whatever topic has happened to take my fancy. Often it has been straight natural history, an account of maybe a saxifrage on Snowdon, a pied flycatcher in the woods, a hawk-moth, an otter, a grass snake, anything I have met with in the previous few days. Or I've been walking the hills or the sea cliffs. Quite often I have ventured into controversial issues and said my say about access to moorlands, forestry, farming, reservoirs, mining in national parks, atomic power stations, the urbanisation of the countryside, the excesses of tourism, low-flying aircraft, over-population, the pet trade, blood sports and so on.

Not all the paper's readers can have loved every word I have written but on the other hand I have made many pen-friends who have kindly kept me informed about their particular corner of nature. Sometimes I have been corrected, as when I reported that I had seen a silver-washed fritillary fly down to lay her eggs on violet leaves in a wood. A reader queried my observation. This butterfly, he said, does not lay her eggs on violet leaves but on the bark of nearby trees. The tiny larvae then have to find their way to violet leaves as best they can, which seems an extraordinary hit-or-miss arrangement. I admitted I had not actually seen the fritillary lay her eggs on violets. I had simply assumed that was why she had dived down into the bracken that covered the woodland floor. When I checked with the books I found my correspondent was quite correct and that I had been caught out in a statement of gross ignorance.

One of my diaries had the luck to stir up an unexpected botanical record. In September, 1962, I was writing about lost alpine plants in Meirionnydd and mentioned that a bush of juniper had been seen on Cader Idris early in the century but not since. This reminded a *Guardian* reader, our friend Dorothy Paish, that her daughter, Veronica, had recently claimed to have seen a juniper on Cader. So now the whole Paish family, it seems, set out for the high cliffs to confirm the record and they duly found the bush again. There it remains, sprawled over a rock above Llyn Aran, and is still the only known specimen of the sub-species *Juniperus communis alpina* anywhere in Meirionnydd, though it is locally common just to the north in Caernarfonshire. I have written in the *Guardian*, probably more than once, about Cader's other famous lost plant, oblong woodsia (*Woodsia ilvensis*), and it is my fervent hope that before I have written my last 'Country Diary' some *Guardian* reader will report that this little fern has also been re-found on Cader Idris. This woodsia, named in honour of the English botanist, Joseph Woods (1776-1864), has been described as Britain's rarest fern. It was found on Cader twice in the late nineteenth century but never since, despite much searching. But Cader is a very big mountain when you are looking for a fern that may be less than two inches long.

On March 13, 1958, in the hope of getting acquainted with a very special wildflower of south Wales, I drove the ninety miles to Swansea. All I knew about the yellow whitlowgrass was that it was not uncommon on the limestone cliffs of Gower, that it grew nowhere else in the British Isles and that it opened in very early spring. The day was not propitious. A cold gale out of the north-west, frequent showers of outsize snowflakes and Swansea's grey industrial landscape made me think of turning back. But deciding that it was too far to go home unrewarded, I took the road for Mumbles, turned up a westward hill and was soon out on the cliffs in yet another brief but blinding blizzard from which I took shelter under an overhang in the rocks.

The squall passed, the sky turned blue and stonechats began sweet warblings in the gorse as I walked on along the cliff-tops. Then without warning, it was snowing again in big wet flakes and again I scurried for shelter under the rocks. Then a patch of bright yellow caught my eye. And that was how, with the snow falling thickly about me, I first saw the yellow whitlowgrass. Though I have seen it since in kinder weather, I remember with affection my first meeting with this beautiful little plant that adorned the snow-covered sea-cliffs of Gower that day like some arctic-alpine on the highest ledges of Snowdon.

The limestone cliffs of south-west Gower where the flora includes the yellow whitlowgrass at its only British locality.

109

The 1950s I think of as my blackcock period. I had seen little of these splendid birds before then and I've hardly seen one since. But when we were living at Felin-y-cwm early in the fifties, the distant bubbling of blackcock was an everyday sound in spring and early summer. Inevitably so, because the southern slopes of Cwm Einion had recently been planted with spruces and larches, just the sort of habitat in which blackcock thrive best. But it doesn't take long in the rains of Wales for young conifers to shoot up and form dense, dark thickets not in the least attractive to blackcock; and so it was that by the end of the fifties the blackcock were already dispersing in search of younger plantations.

Though you may observe displaying blackcock any time of day, the traditional hour to do so is at dawn; and on April 23, 1958, four of us made the effort. They were Penny, myself, Mary Richards (in whose cottage at Brithdir we were staying) and an old friend of Mary's, Frances Pitt of Bridgnorth who had long been one of the most popular writers on British natural history. We got out of bed at 2 a.m. and drove several miles to meet two Forestry Commission workers who had offered to be our guides. Leaving our vehicle we were led up a long, climbing trail through the conifers above Drws-y-nant. A chilly dawn was just breaking as we reached the clearing that was the blackcocks' daily tournament ground. There, crouched behind a thicket of young spruces, we witnessed the pompous dancing, sparring and leaping of the males, and heard all the sneezings, wheezings and bubblings that accompanied these antics. We loved every minute of this adventure. But since those days millions of viewers have seen and heard blackcock performing on television and I doubt if many would wish to be dragged from their beds before dawn to see the real thing.

For over twenty miles a canal winds river-like across the fair county of Montgomery, from Shropshire nearly to Newtown, its water feeding gently in from nearby rivers. Opened in 1821 it soon became busy, the local merchants and farmers thankful to transfer their products from difficult, hilly roads to the placid new waterway. Yet in only a few decades there was talk of abandoning the canal because, parallel to it, had come the railway of 1860. Then as the canal fell into near disuse it began the second phase of its life—as an unintentional nature reserve. No longer disturbed by many barges, the canal became a haven for water plants, some of them rare. There were swarms of fish and therefore many kingfishers. Dragonflies, water beetles, frogs, toads, newts, grass snakes, moorhens and mallard were everywhere. Turtle doves, lesser whitethroats and willow warblers sang along the tow-path hedges in spring. Then came the Second World War and the canal became even more useless to the workaday world because the nearby main road was modernised by replacing its old humpy bridges with level ones that crossed the canal so near to water level that even swans had to duck their heads to get under them, and certainly no boats could pass.

It was my good fortune to become acquainted with this canal when, as a haven for wildlife, it was at its best. I was introduced to it by one of the most enthusiastic naturalists and conservationists Montgomery-shire has ever produced—Janet MacNair of Welshpool (1903-75),

A scene along the Montgomeryshire Canal north-east of Welshpool, 1957.

founder and long the mainstay of the Montgomeryshire Field Society. Primarily a botanist, Janet loved to take people along the canal to show them plants not common elsewhere in Wales, among them frogbit, marsh stitchwort, tubular water-dropwort, flowering rush and the rarer pondweeds. Many of these plants she pointed out to me one summer's day as we followed the canal's winding course through the farmlands.

Today the canal's future is still in doubt but there is popular support for the proposal that those low bridges should once again be raised so that boats may move as they used to, thus creating a holiday playground. Inevitably there are those who shudder at the prospect. Far better, they say, to keep the canal just as it is. Meanwhile, in case it is destined one day to become once again busy with boats, nature reserves are being created alongside it here and there. So whatever happens all will not be lost.

*   *   *

I owe a debt to dear old Evan Roberts of Capel Curig (1909-91). So do we all, all of us who have ever found delight in the mountain plants of Snowdonia, for over many years he was the fountain of all knowledge on the subject. Evan, leaving school at fourteen, spent thirty-three years as a slate-quarry worker high on Moel Siabod, but at the same time he taught himself about plants with such success that he eventually earned his living as a Nature Conservancy botanist and, later still, was given an honorary M.Sc., by the University of Wales. Always eager to help others he became a botanical guru for many of us. A day out with Evan was always memorable, not least for the infectious excitement with which he pointed out the plants of his beloved Eryri.

I have two especially treasured memories of being out with this enraptured man. The first was when he introduced me to the flora of Ogwen. We walked up the rocky path towards Cwm Idwal, then veered left to clamber steeply to the (in those days) seclusion of Cwm Bochlwyd. From there he led us along the ridge called the Gribin and on ever higher to the crags of Cwm Cneifio. For the first time in Britain, I saw moss campion, mountain avens, alpine meadow-rue,

112

Evan Roberts of Capel Curig who had unrivalled knowledge of the mountain plants of Snowdonia. Here he is on the Great Orme, Llandudno.

The Devil's Kitchen cliffs, Cwm Idwal, in Snowdonia, known for three centuries for their alpine plants.

Holly fern, a Snowdon rarity, that was over-collected by Victorian fern-collectors and is still very rare.

alpine bistort, alpine saw-wort and the unique Snowdon lily. I have been a Snowdonia plant enthusiast ever since.

My other outstanding day with Evan Roberts came many years later on the Great Orme, that bold and shapely chunk of limestone that stands into the sea at Llandudno and, though so long a playground for thousands of people, is still splendidly rich in wildflowers. I picked Evan up at Capel Curig but it was not until we reached the Orme and began to look for plants that I realised that he had by now almost completely lost his sight. Was that a handicap for him? Hardly at all. He knew his way about the Orme perfectly and it was fascinating to see him go down on his hands and knees and identify each species by touch: spring cinquefoil, vernal squill, common rockrose, hoary rockrose, kidney vetch and so on. From birth Evan Roberts had been blind in one eye; but with his one good eye he was to find far more plants than most of us manage with two.

In his last years he became completely blind. Yet one day when I called at his house I was told he had gone botanising in the Alps! There, I learned later, he achieved a lifetime ambition. With one of his sons to guide him he saw (or rather touched) the alpine forget-me-not (*Eritrichium nanum*) whose brilliant blue flowers have earned it the title: 'King of the Alps'. 'King of Eryri' would not have been a bad title for Evan Roberts.

⋆   ⋆   ⋆

One day, as the fifties neared their end, there came a gentle knock on our cottage door. I opened it to find our good friend Hubert Mappin, owner of the nearby estate of Ynys-hir that is now well-known as an RSPB Reserve but was then a sequestered private demesne hidden between the main road and the estuary. Hubert Mappin was a diffident, hesitant man, seldom entering into society, being fully occupied with his beautiful estate, his superb garden and his beehives. His reason for coming to see us was most unexpected. One of his farmhouses, Ynys Edwin, had fallen vacant, so would we like to live there?

We had never been to Ynys Edwin but we knew it as a house we could see in the distance on our bird-watching walks to the estuary. To us it was a rather mysterious house, so deeply crouched under its oak-topped hill, so alone at the edge of its peatbog. For days we were undecided, setting pros against cons, but in the end we accepted the invitation. Not the least of our motives was that we sympathised with Hubert Mappin's desire to keep Ynys-hir as a wildlife sanctuary on an estuary much plagued by wildfowl shooting. And we had admired him since the day when, throwing off his shyness, he angrily turned the otter hunt off his river.

Our last day at Felin-y-cwm had a touch of ceremony about it. The day we left we picked a huge bunch of flowers from the garden and took them up to Bwlch Einion, a lonely farmhouse which stood high on the slopes above us and had a huge view north-west to the estuary, Aberdyfi and Cardigan Bay. There lived Tom Jenkins and his mother, and we gave them the flowers for her ninetieth birthday. Mrs Jenkins was of a tough old breed. We had seen her, even in her old age, standing on top of a load of hay, high on a horse-drawn cart, piling up the grass as it was thrown up to her by Tom. Isolated for years in a primeval farmhouse at the end of a long, climbing track, she had the speech, the ways and the thoughts that belonged to a time much earlier than the mid-twentieth century into which she had survived. Penny and I were not the only visitors she had on her ninetieth birthday. Our parish vicar, the poet R. S. Thomas, also walked up to see her. This is his poem for the occasion:

NINETIETH BIRTHDAY

You go up the long track
That will take a car, but is best walked
On slow foot, noting the lichen
That writes history on the page
Of the grey rock. Trees are about you
At first, but yield to the green bracken,
The nightjar's house: you can hear it spin
On warm evenings; it is still now
In the noonday heat, only the lesser
Voices sound, blue-fly and gnat
And the stream's whisper. As the road climbs,
You will pause for breath and the far sea's
Signal will flash, till you turn again
To the steep track, buttressed with cloud.

And there at the top that old woman,
Born almost a century back
In that stone farm, awaits your coming:
Waits for the news of the lost village
She thinks she knows, a place that exists
In her memory only.
             You bring her greeting
And praise for having lasted so long
With time's knife shaving the bone.
Yet no bridge joins her own
World with yours, all you can do
Is lean kindly across the abyss
To hear words that were once wise.

Till the moment of our departure we had doubts about the wisdom of closing the chapter of our life in Cwm Einion. Was it not tempting providence to abandon a place where we had been so contented? To change one's house can be a perilous venture. Many people do it by force of necessity but we were under no such pressure. Yet move we did. The fates were meddling again and life had taken another turn. As we closed Felin-y-cwm gate behind us, Penny quoted a medieval lament from one of her favourite books, *The Wandering Scholars* by Helen Waddell:

> O little house, O dear and sweet our dwelling,
> O little house, for ever fare thee well,
> The trees stand round thee with their
>   sighing branches,
> A little flowering wood for ever fair.
> Small streams about thee...

Chapter 7

So we withdrew from the valley which through most of the fifties had
sheltered us from so many north-east winds. And we came to this
erstwhile farmhouse whose builders of three or four centuries ago
evidently scorned the protection of warm valleys and woodlands, and
were prepared to accept the bleakness of the midwinter estuary where
winds come raging down off the snowfields of the mountains and
gales often leap upon us out of the Atlantic. But there are advantages,
apart from not having any other house in view: even in the depths of
winter, if the clouds unravel, the sun looks at us all day; and behind
us a high, sharp ridge is a shield against winds from the north. All
year round, our southward view is of marshes, then oakwoods, then
the uplands climbing towards Plynlimon which, though not visible,
is always a presence. Often we look that way and see storm clouds
gathering up there. For Plynlimon is a wondrous maker of rain.

Ynys Edwin, our home since 1959.

118

It was, however, not rain but drought which afflicted us in our first year here. 1959 brought us a rare hot summer that blazed on unbelievably week after week. But the spring that preceded it was cool and damp when Penny and I made the move to Ynys Edwin and began our new garden, planting our little azaleas, roses and wheelbarrow-loads of other treasures we brought from Felin-y-cwm. Then came that record-breaking summer. Day by day we watched our well getting ever lower until it was quite dry and we were fetching water from the nearest farm in milk churns. Much in the garden died. It was a disconcerting start to our life in this old house but we consoled ourselves with the thought that people had survived here for centuries and that the well must have dried up many times.

That summer, when even the green fields of Wales looked like Serengeti in the dry season, was a godsend to archaeologists who made new discoveries day after day as the past revealed itself in the form of crop-marks and other signs. Even non-archaeologists like us could clearly see where old, unsuspected walls ran beneath the turf, for above them the grass turned brown much earlier than elsewhere. Those buried walls left us wondering about the people who were here before us long ago; but history doesn't offer so much as a whisper about any of them. Hearsay insists that there have been houses on the site of Ynys Edwin for a huge period of time. But it is only hearsay.

The year we came to live at Ynys Edwin was also the year we got to know an elderly local couple whom we remember with affection. John and Mary Behrend were patrons of art and music and had been especially helpful to Stanley Spencer. Before coming to live in retirement in Wales they had built the memorial chapel, decorated by some of Spencer's best work, at Burghclere in Berkshire; and their house in Machynlleth was full of Spencer's very striking paintings. They loved to talk about him and his work and about Benjamin Britten and Peter Pears who were also close friends of theirs.

That the Behrends lived in a rarified world of art and music so different from our out-door, simple life of nature and gardening did not prevent us from striking up a lasting friendship. One spring day I particularly remember. We were in their house with various of their artistic friends who were deep in aesthetic discussions rather beyond our grasp when, standing by an open window, I thought I caught the

119

notes of a woodlark. When I slipped out I found there was indeed a woodlark circling in full-throated song over the house. I still remember the relief I felt to have escaped for a moment into what was for me the real world, the world of fresh air and singing birds. I am happy also to recall the Behrends' reaction to this little incident: they were touchingly pleased to learn that they had this golden-voiced bird carolling so beautifully above their garden.

*   *   *

On a sunny spring morning in 1960 I stood on a bank of the Severn at Wroxeter near Shrewsbury. The editor of *Country Life* had asked for a topographical article about the road that went with Roman boldness straight to the west across Shropshire and on into Wales; and here I was at the beginning of that road.

By the Severn at Wroxeter (Viroconium or Uriconium) the Romans established an important centre in the territory of the British tribe called the Cornovii. Then after a few decades this military base was allowed to grow into Britain's fourth largest civilian town, Viroconium Cornoviorum. When I saw the high wall of the ruined bath-house, the other traces of the once great town and the square blocks of Roman stone built into the walls of Wroxeter church, Housman's lines inevitably came back to me:

> Today the Roman and his trouble
> Are ashes under Uricon.

By which route the Romans took their westerly way out of Uricon I was not sure but I hoped it was via Atcham, for I wanted to see the Roman stones I had read about in the walls of Atcham church. Sure enough there they were in the north wall as plain to see as those at Wroxeter. Then I stood long on Atcham's seven-arched eighteenth-century bridge over the willow-margined Severn to stare with wonder at what was then one of Britain's largest house martin colonies. It was hypnotising to look down on this throng of graceful, twittering birds, two or three hundred pairs of them, making endless patterns in the air as they dived, climbed, glided, stalled and ballet-danced all day long, coming in and out of their nests so closely crowded along the ledges of the bridge a few feet above the slowly

120

moving river. Sadly it is in the nature of house martin colonies to be unstable and today there is nothing like the number nesting on Atcham's old bridge as there used to be.

From Atcham I drove west without stopping for seventeen miles. The course of the Roman road across Salop is well enough known and I was keen to get to the more mysterious Welsh part of the route. So I came to Westbury where the problems begin. I still have the one-inch-to-the-mile map I had with me that day in 1960. It is dated 1953 and, at six shillings and sixpence, was expensive; but, made of linen, it has proved a good investment. Despite heavy use there still isn't a tear on it, whereas a paper map I bought recently was in tatters after only a few days in the field.

Four miles due west of Westbury, my old one-inch map told me very firmly in capital letters that the ROMAN ROAD climbed up the end of the Long Mountain to proceed boldly south-west along the ridge until it dropped steeply to Forden. So that way I obediently drove. My ears popping, as they always do at about a thousand feet, I came up to meet the fullness of the west wind that sweeps along the level spine of Long Mountain. Up here it was goodbye to hollow lanes and tall hedges and there were wide views of Corndon Hill to the south and the triple head of the Breidden in the north. Ahead was a vast prospect of the upper Severn basin, its myriad fields and little woods vanishing into the blue haze of the Cambrian Mountains.

Thoughts of antiquity persisted on the top of Long Mountain. A rounded breast outlined against the northern sky was labelled 'tumulus' on my map; then there was the Beacon Ring where the banks of a hill-fort are still clear to see despite the wind and the weather of two millennia. Where the road descended to cross the line of Offa's Dyke I diverged to the right into the Leighton estate to see the Royal Forestry Society's famous redwood grove which is one of the most majestic groups of trees in all Britain. It was in 1858 that they were planted by Charles Acker. In their native California the redwoods can live well over two thousand years. On the Long Mountain they may not live so long. But wouldn't it be lovely to come back and see them only five hundred years from now?

Modern experts will not have it that the Roman road ever went over the Long Mountain. Instead they have traced a route along the

121

southern flanks of the hill. No matter, I enjoyed my safari along the top, the singing larks, the sobbing lapwings, the hovering kestrels, the wayside flowers. West of Long Mountain I followed faint hints of an ancient road (gateways, age-old oaks and other signs) across the fields to Forden where the tall-towered church is thought to stand squarely on the Roman road. Then on to Forden Gaer, a well-known Roman camp that is now nothing more than a slightly raised rectangle occupying part of a large pasture.

Deeper into Wales the Roman road, shadowy and faltering over long distances, is plain enough on the approaches to Caersws where the outlines of Roman earthworks are all mixed up with the railway station. From there I went on a good line of scent to the village of Trefeglwys but after that the route passed beyond the conjectural to the realm of fanciful speculation.

I consulted a local expert, C. E. Vaughan Owen, who combined huge learning with total modesty, and together we struck out north-west from Trefeglwys on the assumption that there must have been a link from Caersws to the Roman fort at Pennal at the head of the Dyfi estuary. We had a hilarious day weaving an imaginary Roman road, first up wooded valleys then over treeless hills by way of the hamlet of Staylittle, and so to the derelict lead-mines up at Dylife, mines which were pretty certainly worked by the Romans. At Dylife we also inspected the hill-top site of what archaeologists have identified as a Roman signalling station. There we abandoned the quest, resolving to return one day and trace the road to Pennal. Alas, we never did.

*   *   *

In those years I was getting more and more involved in writing and broadcasting; and also in lecturing to extra-mural classes in natural history, with the result that I eventually gave up schoolmastering. For several years I was out most evenings, October to March, addressing groups at various centres from Aberystwyth to Oswestry. I enjoyed facing groups of adults. Their questions were often very searching and I found I had to study and think about natural history problems which would never otherwise have occurred to me. Class members were frequently more knowledgeable than I was in their special fields of interest, and learning was often a two-way process. There was also the bonus that among those who came to the classes I made many lasting friends.

In early June 1960, Penny and I set off on a brief tour of Anglesey with David and Dorothy Paish, two keen botanists and gardeners who were members of my extra-mural class at Welshpool. We drove by way of Dolgellau and made our first stop at a botanically intriguing old copper mine amid the conifers of Coed y Brenin. Here, on spoil heaps of mysterious ecology, flourishes a strangely mixed community of plants like thrift, vernal sandwort, fairy flax and broad-leaved helleborine. Then to Barmouth where we found the shy little fern, lanceolate spleenwort, in a roadside wall. Then up the coast to Llanbedr to camp in the garden of our friends the Stringers who promised to show us a hoopoe at eight o'clock the following morning, which they duly did. It had been thus punctual every day for a week, perching on precisely the same bare tree-top to shout *oop-oop-oop* outside the farmhouse at Gelli-las.

A wild part of the north coast of Anglesey—the view east from Dinas Gynfor near Cemaes.

We called at Morfa Harlech sand dunes where there were hundreds of green-winged orchids nearly over and southern marsh orchids just opening. We camped that night at the foot of Bwrdd Arthur, a flat-topped hill of limestone which looks over the sea near the north-east corner of Anglesey. Next day on this 'Arthur's Table' we were happy amongst all the limestone plants we are so starved of in our part of north Ceredigion: early purple orchid, columbine, salad burnet, bloody cranesbill and common and hoary rockroses alongside what seemed to be hybrids between the two. Dingy skippers were prominently on the wing amongst yellow mats of birdsfoot trefoil, their food-plant. The next day was spent at the fen called Gors Goch and we went to sleep listening to little owls, nightjars, grasshopper warblers and the bleating of snipe. I won't list the huge number of plants we found there next day, both calcicole and calcifuge. Among those quite new to us I especially remember marsh fern and pale heath violet.

We moved west along the coast to Cemlyn and found a wondrous extent of sea kale in full white flower on the top of a curving shingle beach. But terns, ringed plovers and oystercatchers were at their nests and we did not disturb them. Linnets passed in twittering bands, stonechats scolded and lark-song filled the sky. Next day we climbed the rocky flanks of Holyhead Mountain but did not find its prize plant, the annual rockrose, until it was mostly shedding its petals, which it does rather punctually about midday. Its last petals dropped even as I took its photograph. We watched seabirds on South Stack's ancient, distorted cliffs, then followed the south coast to camp just east of Aberffraw close to the miniature church of Llangwyfan which stands solitary on an off-shore rock to which we walked at low tide. In the evening a short-eared owl flew by our camp and partridges called in the fields. I wonder if there are partridges there still?

It is no distance from Aberffraw to the pine plantations of Newborough. We walked through the trees to the plant-rich, moist hollows in the dunes. A male Montagu's harrier rolled lightly across the scene (they nested there annually in those days but were often robbed by collectors). We saw countless marsh orchids of many colours and sizes. The grass of Parnassus was beginning to open (is there any more elegant a flower?). We walked through bright-blue spreads of viper's bugloss; and at Llanddwyn there was sea-lavender along the cliff ledges, sea bindweed in the sand and that sinister plant, henbane, on waste ground by the old coastguard cottages. We came home from Anglesey in the full knowledge that we had seen only the smallest fraction of what was clearly a wonderful county for naturalists.

That summer I went to give a talk to a Holiday Fellowship group at Llandogo in Gwent, prior to leading them on a nature walk next day. To refresh my memory of that part of the lower Wye I drove there on the previous day, for I wanted to sort out a route for our outing through the wooded hills. As it was windstill, warm and dry that first night, there was no need of a tent and I slept under the stars at the edge of a peatbog near Trelleck with the scent of pines all round me and the purring of several nightjars.

Next day I was delighted to find that my fellow speaker was Emrys G. Bowen, Professor of Geography at Aberystwyth. Bowen was my idea of what a university teacher ought to be—someone happy to emerge from the cloisters and come amongst the people. He believed passionately in taking education into the furthermost recesses of society. But he was not just an extra-mural lecturer (you are paid to be that). At the drop of a piece of chalk he would travel far, often on wintry nights, to address (in Welsh or English) any group no matter how small—Young Farmers' Clubs, Womens Institutes, Merched y Wawr and a great many besides, often at his own expense. He could talk on an infinity of topics for he was not only a geographer but also a historian of repute. His lecture on the drovers and their roads was famous but he was equally at home on Celtic saints, the history of Llanbadarn Fawr, Welsh emigration to America, phenology and almost any subject you could think of. I never saw anyone more at home on a lecture platform. He spoke with wit and sparkle and with never a hint of hesitation, self-consciousness or affectation. His voice was clipped and clear and with his friendly and familiar style he was always on the same level as his audience, children as well as adults. It was fascinating to hear his facts and thoughts come forth with perfect orderliness and timing. In all his lectures I never saw him refer to any notes.

On a beautiful morning I led my party up through the trees above Llandogo, pointing out birds, insects and plants. As it was mid-June, bird-song had mostly fallen away but I was relieved to hear the wood warbler still in good voice, for this is a bird little known to many novice bird-watchers, especially those coming from some parts of England. A redstart was still muttering a few notes up in the leaves but for all we saw of him we might as well have been in a tropical rainforest. The plants were easier. In those limestone woods we found plenty of wood spurge, stinking iris, mood melick, soft shieldfern, hartstongue, rusty-back fern, wood spotted orchid, twayblade, guelder rose, dogwood, common buckthorn and many others.

We made our way up the steep slopes of Beacon Hill and on the thousand-foot summit we even found a few bluebells still lingering. We also came upon a wood ants' nest—a huge pile of conifer needles pullulating with large brown ants to-ing and fro-ing with their treasures of food and nesting material. Trying the old experiment to show that ants' nests have very acid interiors, we buried a bluebell spike in this nest. When we pulled it out after ten minutes the flowers had turned pink just like litmus paper. From there, by lanes and footpaths, we descended through woods and across fields to the Wyeside ruins of Tintern Abbey where the ground was decked with the little pink flowers of shining cranesbill.

It was also in the summer of 1960, on a day out with the West Wales Field Society, that I first saw a gwyniad, a fish so Welsh that you will hear no other name for it until you get to the English Lake District, where it is a schelly, or to southern Scotland where they call it a powan. We were introduced to the fishy richness of Llyn Tegid (Bala Lake) by Dr E. W. Jones of Liverpool University who took us out in a boat with a gill net. The gwyniad, we learnt, lived in shoals in the colder layers of this deep lake, feeding on such minute lifeforms that it seldom shows any interest in anglers' lures. It can be netted, however, as our leader demonstrated. Down went the net and soon up came two very lively gwyniads, silvery beauties about a foot long, superficially herring-like but really of the salmon cousinhood.

Also netted with our two gwyniaid (to use the Welsh plural) was a grayling, a surprise to me because I had thought of grayling as river dwellers which I had seen people fishing for in the Lugg in Herefordshire and in the Monnow in Gwent. Dr Jones told of other fish in the lake, ranging in size from salmon to roach, eels, lampreys, stone loaches, bullheads and minnows. But apart from the gwyniad, the fish for which this water has long been famous are its great pike, trout and perch. In recent years rudd and silver bream have been added to the fishy multitude.

So we learnt that Llyn Tegid is much more than a smiling lake nearly four miles long with green hills all round. It is a profound and healthful water that for thousands of years has been home for several million native fish, their individual life-styles all interacting and evolving naturally and robustly together. We must make sure that this rich underwater world, of which there is no equal elsewhere in Wales, will never be brought to disaster by direct human interference, acid rain or any other form of pollution.

*   *   *

One of the joys of living near the estuary is the spring flighting of the shelducks. Perhaps we are working in the garden one morning in early April when we hear vibrant quackings and delicious whistlings overhead; we look up to see the year's first mating flight of maybe half-a-dozen of these almost goose-sized black and white ducks. From then onwards the world is different: we have new neighbours and the shelducks have a new life. Day after day they quit the estuary to perform these morning and sometimes evening flights, always soon circling back to the salt marshes.

Then one day their internal clocks go *ping* and their routine changes. As they wheel round over the woods there comes a moment when they stall in mid-flight and go fluttering down through the oaks to stand together in a glade. Here is their trysting place, here they will look for suitable rabbit-holes in which to hide their nests and here they will go through their strange ceremonies and displays. So these colourful fowl of the open shore and the sea winds become birds of the woods as well; and they will keep up this dual life-style until it is early summer and their newly hatched ducklings have to be led down to their estuary feeding grounds, a journey that may be long and dangerous.

A quandary faced by some shelducks is when they have to bring their brood to the estuary across a trafficky highway and find that the way is blocked by a wall on the other side of the road. This is a panicky situation in which the ducklings dash about all over the road and can easily get run over. Some motorists stop and help them over the wall where the parents soon collect them. Others, just as well-meaning, collect the ducklings, take them home and try to rear them, mistakenly believing them to have been abandoned by their parents. One day a motorist, driving along the estuary road from Aberdyfi, picked up eleven such 'lost' babies and delivered them to the police station at Machynlleth. Our Machynlleth police are always pretty resourceful but to care for infant shelducks is rather outside their remit. What they did know was that our vicar, R. S. Thomas, was a bird-enthusiast; and so it came about that he and his wife found themselves foster-parents of a difficult family.

It was difficult because of the problem of what to feed them on, these day-old ducklings whose natural food is minute forms of invertebrate life that live in the muds of estuaries. A farmer advised chicken meal but the ducklings began to die. There followed very harrowing days as infant mortality got worse. When an SOS went to Peter Scott at Slimbridge the telegraphed reply was: 'Try turkey food'. By this time only four infants survived. But the turkey diet, so much richer in vitamins, did the trick. They thrived miraculously and a few weeks later I had the satisfaction of going to the estuary with R. S. Thomas and releasing four full-sized young shelducks at a spot where they soon joined a passing flotilla of others of their kind.

*　　　*　　　*

Among Welsh people there is a tradition of climbing Snowdon by moonlight in the hope of seeing the sunrise from the summit. When it started I have no idea but I like to think it may be a throw-back to some ancient pantheistic phase in the evolution of the Celtic mind. For these convivial ascents by moonlight the route seems usually to have been the track from Llanberis. People used to come from far away to join in these frolics, even parties of the Liverpool Welsh arriving at Caernarfon by train and then changing for Llanberis in the days before the Llanberis line was closed.

Only once have I climbed Snowdon by moonlight. I went up from the south side. On a September evening in 1960 the moon rose clear above my tent in Nant Gwynant and I could not resist her invitation. In soft moonlight I clambered up through the boulders and loose scree of the Watkin Path, a scramble of which I recall little except that somewhere high up I disturbed a little party of ring ouzels which were roosting among the stones. They flew off into the moonlight with spluttering cries.

Even on the mountain-top it was windless; and the moon was still brilliant as I got into my sleeping bag. I lay a while thinking of those who had come up here by night, not only the merry parties of young Welsh people but also the more sober English travellers of the Romantic period who aspired to pen sunrise lyrics on the summit. I slept in the shelter of a rock and remember nothing of the night except that I was joined by a couple of sheep about 2 a.m. So passed the only night in my life when I have slept between two sheep. I hope they were as comfortable as I was.

Next morning I saw no sunrise. By dawn Snowdon's usual morning cloud had come in off the sea; but I lay there enjoying the mountain silence. The *kronk-kronk* of ravens waking from their sleep was the only sound I heard in the clammy dawn. And all the way down the Watkin Path there was not a sign of life except when I was startled by a loud burst of song that came from one of the wrens which live among the mountain rocks. At the slate-quarry ruins I watched a pair of choughs walking tamely about, pecking into the turf, quickly flirting out their wings every time they called out their distinctive *chee-ow, chee-ow*. Here I was clear of the cloud at last and, with wheatears and pipits as my companions, I came down into the sunshine of a warm September day.

I like to think of Sir Edward Watkin, creator of the Watkin Path. He was the man who went to Dover in 1882 and started to build the Channel Tunnel. He had got less than a mile when he was stopped by the Government who bowed to the public furore stirred up by politicians claiming that such a tunnel would be a threat to national security. So instead of spending his wealth on a tunnel, Sir Watkin came and bought the south side of Snowdon which was up for sale in 1889. Was he, I wonder, persuaded by the pre-sale eloquence of the auctioneer who said: 'Consider the enjoyment you will be able to give to thousands: the fishing, the climbing of the mountainsides, the marvellous views and the joy of allowing the people freely to ramble all over the place. There are few opportunities ever afforded a man to possess an estate, a park like this, and know that the people are all able to enjoy it without paying a farthing for it'. So, back in the nineteenth century, the national park idea was beginning to stir in people's minds; and Sir Watkin made a good start in September 1892 when he opened his now famous path up Snowdon in the presence of 83-year-old Prime Minister Gladstone and a multitude of people.

Chapter 8

The first of March is a very special day in Wales. It is Gŵyl Ddewi, St David's Day, when some people wear daffodils in their button-holes. It also happens to be my birthday and occasionally I have celebrated it by going off in search of wild daffodils, or Lent lilies, as they are often called. But not every year are wild daffodils showing really well by Gŵyl Ddewi. To achieve that they need mild weeks beforehand such as we were blessed with in 1961 which produced one of my best daffodil birthdays.

Guided by Salter's flora of Cardiganshire I decided that the fertile valley of the Aeron offered the nearest hope of success. The last day of February had been wet and gloomy but March came in full of radiance from dawn onwards. After some unrewarding searches along the main Aeron river I came to a wet-floored dingle by a tributary rill; and there, under a scrub of birch and hazel, were wild daffodils in plenty among the triangular leaves of wild arums. In such a spot, in the far west of Wales, more than a little doubt must creep in as to whether these daffodils are true natives or not. The Welsh may have taken the daffodil to their hearts but, compared with some parts of England, Wales on the whole is not good daffodil country. What must add to the doubt about those Aeron valley daffodils is that among them were several clumps of snowdrops; and few botanists accept snowdrops as native anywhere in Britain. So whoever had put snowdrops there might well have planted wild daffodils too. Not that such anxieties afflicted me on Gŵyl Ddewi, 1961. The sun was shining and the daffodils were at perfection. What more could I ask for on my birthday?

I also count it among my blessings that I once spent two whole days on the Pembrokeshire coast with Tommie Warren Davis, then the outstanding naturalist of those parts. Tommie was an all-rounder. Primarily a botanist, he also took on board birds, mammals, insects and pretty well everything else in nature. He had a voice that often stammered, an eye that winked at you disconcertingly and an enthusiasm that was boundless. In his company you needed to be ever on your toes, so quickly did his conversation switch from plants to butterflies, moths, frogs, foxes, fulmars, otters, seals and so on. His friends despaired about his grasshopper-mindedness, fearing it would prevent him from finishing his great project, a flora of Pembrokeshire. And yes, in the end he died with the work far from completed. But nothing anyone could have said would ever have changed this delightful, youthfully eager man who so loved wild Pembrokeshire and wanted to miss nothing of its delights. We must be thankful that although he did not accomplish a full-length flora, he did produce, in 1970, a very good interim list of the county's plants.

In the spring of 1961 I stayed with him in his house at St Ishmael where he first of all took me on a tour of his parish churchyard to show me how rich it was in plants both wild and cultivated. Then off we went on a round of south-west Pembrokeshire, looking at lovely woods along the Eastern Cleddau river, then the flowery old limestone quarries of West Williamston. Eventually we came to the battle-torn desolation of the Castlemartin artillery range which we were able to cross because it was a public holiday. Soon we were out on wild limestone sea cliffs where wheatears threw themselves into the air in courtship display as we walked out to the great promontory of St Govan's. It was a breezy, sun-filled day with a heavenly light on the sea and sparkling rollers bursting up the cliffs. We passed the banks and ditches of a cliff-edge fortress of prehistory, hoping that there had been more peace in the lives of the Iron Age people than is suggested by all the defence works they have left behind them. We skirted round a vast blow-hole at the bottom of which the sea was booming and boiling and Tommie told me of a day he had been there when a hurricane was causing the sea to explode out of this horrendous shaft, throwing up showers of stones and spume like an erupting volcano.

From St Govan's we went to Bosherston and its three long-fingered lily ponds that stretch inland from the beach and look perfectly natural but which were in fact creations of the Stackpole estate that covers all this part of the coast and now, mercifully, belongs to the National Trust. We were too early for the water lilies—they are flowers of the summer and only their green and purple leaves were showing. But there were yellow irises, cowslips, primroses and an abundance of twayblades. Also early purple orchids, arum lilies, soft shieldferns and hartstongues; tall blue aquilegias and short blue vernal squills; wild privet, salad burnet and a tangle of the wild clematis that is called old man's beard because of its tousled, grey seed-heads. That spring, holly blues were amongst the commonest butterflies. A grass snake swam across one of the pools. Webs of lackey-moth caterpillars, defiantly blue and red, were draped over the bushes.

Next day we went to Marloes and walked round the Deerpark cliffs from Martinshaven to Gateholm. We looked across to the islands of Skokholm and Skomer where white-edged azure seas were breaking all along the rocks. We passed through bright-yellow sheets of kidney vetch, white cushions of sea campion, pink carpets of thrift. Tommie showed me the peculiar habit of the broom of those cliffs: instead of growing upright it lays its yellow sprays upon the ground, spread out like the spokes of a wheel. A bright-green bed of golden samphire, not yet in flower, draped a patch of the rocks.

Choughs called musically as they played in the wind as only choughs can. Larks sang high in the blue, stonechats scolded from gorse-tops and at times the air was 'full of the linnet's wings'. (Yeats's poems are ever in the back of my mind.) It was a day of migration: every few minutes swallows, house martins, sand martins and occasionally a swift, passed north close to the cliff-tops. There was no mistaking the urgency of their purpose. We followed them round the great curve of St Bride's Bay. At Newgale was the only sea-cliff heronry I have ever seen. At St David's we went down to Caerbwdi Bay where Tommie wanted to show me the purple cliffs from which stone was quarried in the Middle Ages for the building of the cathedral.

We ended the day on the wild, rock-scattered slopes that go out to St David's Head. Across a gully we examined through binoculars a prosperous patch of roseroot in an inaccessible fissure high in the cliffs, a plant I had never before seen except on mountain ledges. We saw Arthur's Quoit, a Neolithic chambered tomb; and hut circles, walls, and field systems which are perhaps of the Iron Age. We looked across to the whole of Ramsey Island with its shapely hills. And as the light faded we stood at the tip of St David's Head, watching the sea as wave after wave of shearwaters, only just visible in the gloom, came skimming northwards, low over the water, heading for Bardsey Island or fishing grounds in Cardigan Bay.

A few weeks later I was with a party leaping off seaweedy rocks into Alf Knowles's boat at Martinshaven on our way to Skomer. It was my first visit to that finest of all Welsh bird islands with its precious community of shearwaters, puffins, gulls, kittiwakes, guillemots and razorbills. The tameness of the puffins amazed us. A flotilla of them surrounded the boat as we came in to the landing place. Others whirred round us or stood in groups and looked at us calmly as we climbed a zigzag path to the level top of the island. It was the same on the great cliffs of the Wick; groups of two or three dozen stood on the rocky slopes above the sea, some holding bunches of little silvery fish in their colourful beaks. Later Alf Knowles took us all round the island by boat and again we experienced unbelievable tameness—this time it was kittiwakes sitting unmoved on seaweed nests only a few feet above us. Looking up those sheer cliffs at rank above rank of those beautiful small gulls of the ocean, I thought how right it is that man has ceased to farm this island or exploit its rabbits and has handed it over to its rightful owners—the birds of the sea.

South from Skomer the next island is Skokholm which I made several attempts to get to from Dale Fort before I succeeded. Milford Haven may be perfectly smooth when you set out; but once you are round the shelter of St Ann's Head you are in another world where the sea can play tricks with little boats even on days of near calm. Once we got all the way to the island but then found ourselves tossing up and down the wall of the landing place with such violence we had to turn back. I finally set foot there on a perfect spring day when, astonishing sight if you are not used to those islands, Skokholm's plateau was a sheet of bluebells all in flower; and amongst them gleaming white gulls sat serenely on their well-spaced nests.

Rabbits abounded, Skokholm's uniquely flea-less rabbits that never catch myxomatosis because it is a flea-borne disease. There were swards where the turf was so closely rabbit-nibbled that it truly was as smooth as a billiard table. Yet elsewhere there were patches blue with vernal squill and ground ivy or yellow with celandines. Many of those who stay at the island's bird observatory go to see the migrants of spring and autumn. In the breeding season there are pipits, wheatears and skylarks; there are the diurnal seabirds of the cliffs and, after dark, huge numbers of storm petrels and shearwaters. To spend part of a night with them is one of the experiences every birdwatcher ought to have at least once. It adds a dimension to existence to be on this wild, windswept rock out in the isolation of the sea and feel the close presence of a multitude of unseen birds all about you in the darkness.

1961 turned out to be a year of islands; and for one week of my life I got as near as ever I will to becoming an archaeologist. This was when Douglas Hague and his team from the Royal Commission on Ancient Monuments were carrying out a dig on St Tudwal's East Island off Aber-soch along the Llŷn peninsula. Douglas, who had a nice sense of humour, invited me to join them as 'the expedition's ornithologist'. So on the morning of August 2, I looked across from the nearest headland to the pair of St Tudwal's isles that guard the

Archaeologists on St. Tudwal's East Island near Pwllheli, north Wales, August 1961.

bay at Aber-soch. They stood a mile apart, high, treeless, flattish domes girded by dark-grey cliffs. Beyond them the whole sweep of Cardigan Bay faded into the haze of Pembrokeshire. On the East Island (sometimes called the blind island because, unlike West Island, it has no lighthouse) I could see the coloured tents of the archaeologists who were braving the weather (they needed bravery in that stormy summer) in order to dig into the remains of a medieval religious community of whose history little was known.

A boat took me to the island on the calmest of seas. Yet such are the tricks of the coastal weather that I had only just got my tent pitched amongst the others when quite a fierce wind sprang out of the south-west and a mournful bell began to ring, a bell attached to a nearby buoy and plainly warning of storm. I thought of those legendary lands lost under the waters of Cardigan Bay and of the drowned villages whose church bells are said to be audible as they ring under the sea in times of heavy weather. The wind blew itself out during the night and my first morning on the island was still and warm. Then quite suddenly the afternoon brought a real gale which raged all night and Douglas and I stayed up through all the hours of darkness looking after the tents, knocking in pegs and adding supplementary ropes. Mercifully no damage was done.

In the tranquil weather of the rest of the week I kept an eye on the birds, hoping for early migrants but they were very few: terns in small convoys, an occasional tittering whimbrel, a very lost-looking willow warbler totally out of place on an island whose only cover was a meagre patch of nettles. On the cliffs there were herring gulls and about a hundred pairs of kittiwakes with their young. In crevices I was pleased to find the sea spleenwort, a fern which, more than all others, enjoys the kiss of the salt sea breezes.

At times I watched the diggers at their work, two dozen earnest people, mostly young, delving away in the sunshine, spading out the story of past time. This was the second year of the dig and by the time of my arrival they were deep into an ancient subsoil where their tools had made contact with stones laid there many centuries ago. Here the work went more carefully. The spade was forsaken for the trowel as the squared faces of what seemed to be altar stones came to light. Someone found a fragment of pottery, someone else the line of a

Kittiwakes nesting on St. Tudwal's East Island, August 1961.

drain. Then three graves were exposed near the altar and as they were uncovered we saw three pairs of leg bones begin to appear side by side. To examine these the tools were a delicate knife and a tiny brush. For in six hundred years the bones, some yellowed, some blackened, had become soft to the touch.

So, day after day, the patient work continued on that slope above the sea while the wind played in the tall grasses and blew scuds across the blue water. Yachts often sailed by below us, their occupants looking up wonderingly, perhaps taking us to be some sort of penal settlement. Seals also watched us from the water, showing no fear, only curiosity. Many times a day gannets, huge and gleaming white, passed close to the island, often diving into the sea with a splash of white water. I have one regret about my stay on St Tudwal's: that it had not taken place decades earlier. For then we would have had the company of a vast throng of nesting puffins by day and a great caterwauling colony of shearwaters at night. Alas, by 1961, all these splendid fowl had long ago deserted the island, no one is sure why.

*　　*　　*

The following winter (1961-62) was very sharp for several weeks. We had had days of mildness and December sunshine. In the garden both song and mistle thrushes sang and *Prunus subhirtella* had produced a miracle of pale-pink flowers. Yet suddenly on the fourteenth, out on the estuary counting the birds, we found ourselves in a freezing gale from the east. The commonest bird that day was the wigeon in several groups, making 1,200 in all. The cold continued and on Boxing Day the estuary froze right across at the narrowest neck. By December 28 the Severn was reported frozen at Shrewsbury; and so also was the Avon at Bath for the first time anyone could recall. As December turned to January our estuary was piled from end to end with ice-floes. They drifted slowly up with the tide, crackling as they broke their edges against each other. When the tide ebbed some of the ice was carried out to sea but much of it was left stranded along the saltings like block scree on a mountain. All waders, ducks and geese had gone. The wigeon were reported miles down the coast, rafts of them floating on the sea like scoters.

By January 2 some land birds were getting feeble. Redwings fluttered weakly in village gardens. Song thrushes became very tame. A bullfinch and a pied wagtail were brought to us emaciated. Curlews came to feed in the field by our garden gate. So did lapwings. On the estuary reed buntings, linnets and greenfinches were surviving on the seeds of the cord-grass (*Spartina*). It froze harder than ever and snow fell in heavy showers. The thaw did not come till January 5 and at first it was slow. Though the snow gradually vanished, the frost was still deep in the ground and we knew there would be heavy losses among the garden plants. Then suddenly it was misty and mild. The ice melted from the estuary and by January 8 the wigeon were all back. The curlews and lapwings had gone from outside the garden gate, our pair of buzzards were circling and calling over their nesting wood. The world was back to normal. We planted our shallots.

*　　*　　*

I have lately been bereaved of one of my oldest friends, Francis Peach of Lichfield, whose parents lived in retirement at Aberystwyth. Francis and his father, both ardent birdwatchers, often came to the Dyfi estuary in the fifties to see the ducks, waders and hen harriers. Francis always kept a careful life-list of birds and could tell you at any moment what his tally was. Yet he rarely went out of his way to see a new bird, being content to add fresh names to his list whenever they happened to turn up in the normal way of holidays at home and abroad. So when he died his score was not at all phenomenal; though, at 1,020, it was quite respectable.

One memory of Francis that I treasure is of when his father died at Aberystwyth in April, 1962, and was cremated at Shrewsbury, forty miles away. Francis took his binoculars with him and was delighted, as the cortege passed the Breidden Hills, to see a male sparrowhawk circling in courtship display. (Sparrowhawks, be it remembered, had become quite scarce by 1962 because of toxic chemicals on the land.) Francis told me afterwards that maybe people were shocked to see him carrying binoculars at a funeral. 'But', he said, 'I know Pop would have been shocked at the idea of my *not* taking my binoculars on a journey right across Wales!'

Sparrowhawks were much in our minds that year because a pair bred nearer to our house than ever before or since. Penny and I have always admired sparrowhawks and we felt honoured to have this pair nesting so close that as we gardened that June we could hear the shrill hunger cries of the young getting louder day by day. In the first week of July the young swallows began to leave their nests in our out-buildings and the air was alive with them as they fluttered weakly about on their maiden flights. Then the male sparrowhawk came, greeted by shrieks of alarm from the parent swallows. He glided quite slowly in amongst the hovering young swallows, picked one up almost gently and took it away with the same leisurely pace with which he had arrived. These forays were repeated so many times that I don't care to think what heavy losses the swallows suffered.

Watching our swallows being taken day after day was a severe test of our devotion to hawks. We greatly loved our Ynys Edwin swallows, for this was the first house we had lived in where we could wake up every morning from April to September and hear their lively songs close to our windows. So if we could have protected them from the hawks we surely would have done so. In the first week of August I went across the pasture to the sparrowhawk wood. I looked up at their saucer of a nest high in a larch but it was now empty and the trees were silent all round. The hawks had gone away on their late-summer wanderings. In our buildings the swallows were now ready to launch their second broods into the air. This time there would be no hawks to worry them; and the parent swallows had long forgotten their losses of July. We alone remembered.

*   *   *

Those of us who live in a land of acid soils are unlikely ever to forget any encounter with a rich limestone flora. So it was for me on June 15, 1962, when I was shown the delights of Llanymynech Hill near Oswestry by three local enthusiasts, Doris Pugh, Mary Hignett and Gwyneth Jones. We made a long list of plants, the calcicoles along with all the rest. But inevitably it is the calcicoles that stay in the mind: the riot of old man's beard and black bryony scrambling over everything; thickets of dogwood, spindle, guelder rose and spurge laurel; an abundance of marjoram, crosswort, rockrose, yellow-wort and salad burnet; more shyly, herb paris, globe-flower and stinking hellebore. And a delight of orchids: frog, greater butterfly, twayblade, bee, green-winged, early purple and many broad-leaved helleborines. I have returned to this splendid hill several times since but that first eye-opening visit stands out clearest in my memory.

Next month I was again involved with lime-loving plants but in a very different setting. I was near the summit of Moelwyn Mawr which keeps a watchful eye on the slate-quarry town of Blaenau Ffestiniog. All the way up, the rocks looked acid and bare and where there was any vegetation it was mostly heather and bilberry, the 'flora of poverty' as the Rev John Evans put it when he came this way in 1798. Suddenly my luck changed. What was I looking at if it wasn't a patch of green spleenwort, brittle bladder fern and mountain sorrel, all plants of limestony places? Better still, I found a few sparse flowers of a very local alpine, the northern rockcress (*Cardaminopsis petraea*).

I knew that Edward Lhuyd had reported northern rockcress from somewhere on this range in the late seventeenth century. What luck, I thought, if I were the first to see it there since then! But when I looked up the records I found that it had been reported by James Backhouse in the 1870s and David Angell Jones some years later, both of them eminent plantsmen. The first to discover northern rockcress in Britain was Thomas Johnson who called it *Nasturtium petraea*. He found it on Snowdon in 1639, no doubt on Clogwyn Du'r Arddu where it is so abundant, an admirable plant to see clinging to sheer cliffs and nonchalantly facing all the winds that blow. When John Ray included it in his *Synopsis* of British plants of 1696 he gave a nod of acknowledgement to its finder by calling it 'Dr Johnson's rock-cresse' and it is sad that the name has not been kept to remind us of a pioneer botanist not otherwise commemorated in British plant names in English, Latin or Welsh.

It is difficult not to feel sorry for this Dr Johnson 'citizen and apothecarye of London' (he got the 'Dr' as an honorary degree from Oxford). He came all the way to Wales along those dreadful seventeenth-century roads, had just one day on Snowdon and it rained. Then a few days later when he came down the coast by way of Harlech and Barmouth the weather was still atrocious and he was soaked to the skin by the time he got to Machynlleth. Here, however, he found welcome and comfort before going on next day to Montgomery. Despite our rain he was full of plans to come herborising in Wales again 'when the weather looks more promising and I'm not so pressed for time'. But five years later, fighting for the King in the Civil War in 1644, he got a bullet in the shoulder in a skirmish in Hampshire and died a fortnight later. He has left us a list of his more interesting finds on Snowdon. Top of it is his *Nasturtium petraea*.

In a letter of November 24, 1696, Edward Lhuyd reported on a visit to what was evidently Clogwyn Du'r Arddu, the cliff where Johnson had discovered his rock-cress. Among Lhuyd's finds that day he mentions 'plenty of the *Nasturtium petraea* of Johnson'. So whenever I see the northern rock-cress showing its mass of little white flowers on Clogwyn in June I think of Lhuyd there in 1696 thinking of Johnson there fifty-seven years earlier. In fact botanical ghosts are ever with us on these plant-rich crags. No matter how chilly the rain or how slippery the rocks, we can take encouragement from the spirits of Johnson, Ray, Willughby, Lhuyd, Brewer, Richardson, Dillenius and others who came scrambling up these same ledges in the hope of finding something new or rare. They did not always succeed. Witness William Bingley, a century after Lhuyd; he had been told just where to see the alpine woodsia fern but he ended in despair: 'I fought for it feveral times, but in vain'. All botanists know just how he felt. It was at Clogwyn Du'r Arddu that William Bingley unintentionally made history. A twenty-four-year-old student on vacation from Oxford, Bingley was accompanied by a fellow plant enthusiast, thirty-three-year-old Peter Williams, rector of Llanberis. One day in 1798 they were examining the alpines that grow along the skirts of the great vertical precipice. Then they looked up and wondered what plants might be found on the higher ledges. Curiosity overcame any fears they may have had and they ventured up a gully which goes slanting up the cliff to form one of the arms of that huge downfold in the rocks that is easily seen by passengers on the Snowdon trains. Up and up they scrambled, happily collecting their specimens, until they chanced to look down and came near to panic when they realised what a drop there was below them and how much more difficult it is to climb down than to climb up. They decided that their best hope was to try and find a way to the top; and with Williams using his belt to help Bingley over the tricky bits, they eventually came safely out of trouble. Their heroic scramble has come to be regarded as the first rock-climb in Britain. So if Bingley could have seen what was to be said of him years later in the *Dictionary of National Biography* he would surely have been surprised to read: 'His life was devoid of incident'!

If botanising on Snowdonia's mountain cliffs is a total delight it is because here is a rich flora which has changed little for three hundred years (and a thousand years before that?). It is true that some of the rarities were ravaged by Victorian collectors. The holly fern, for instance, was nearly wiped out and is only now beginning very slowly to recover. But on the whole, when I started to look at Snowdonian alpines under the tutelage of Evan Roberts, the community of mountain plants was robustly intact, as it is to this day.

It was a far less happy story down in the valleys. Beside the destruction of the herb-rich meadows we also saw in the 1960s many a broad-leaved wood being cut down and replaced by conifers. Even more excruciating was to see that in woods where the oaks were uneconomic to cut down and clear away, they had rings cut deep into their bark so that they died on their feet with newly planted conifers growing up all round them. The sight of those vandalised oaks, some more than two centuries old, is one of the saddest memories of those years. Mercifully present-day forest practices are more in tune with care of the natural environment. In some areas considerable improvements are taking place: streamsides are being cleared of conifers and more broad-leaved trees are now planted or allowed to regenerate spontaneously. Sadly, vast spruce plantations continue to spread across some of Britain's moorlands, especially in Scotland. My thoughts about them, like the plantations themselves, grow ever gloomier.

The utter wrongness of mass plantations of alien conifers came home to me with the sharpest shock when Penny and I got to the mountains of East Africa in 1963. There we were shown a high plateau that was the most flowery place we had ever seen, a plant-rich natural meadow going on for miles in all directions, coloured everywhere with orchids, red-hot pokers, asters and scores of other delights. But outlined ominously on the horizon were small blocks of pines from all over the world that were being grown experimentally to find out which would most quickly and efficiently obliterate all that marvellous spread of native flora. A few days later we visited an area that had already gone under the conifer blanket. This was a mountain rich in deep, ultra-fertile, volcanic soils. Seeing that folded landscape deep in pines from other continents I asked myself, not for the first time, if it could possibly be right to go on for ever changing the vegetation of the world. Surely enough damage has already been done?

★   ★   ★

Though we thought we had had a bad winter in 1961-2, the next was far worse. It was a long, severe freeze-up lasting on and off from late December 1962 to early March 1963. On the shore there were

143

shellfish by the thousand lying frozen to death along the tide-line all the thirty miles from Borth to Harlech and no doubt far beyond. Gulls, crows and ravens had a wonderful time feeding on all this carrion; but most other birds suffered, especially the usually vulnerable ones such as redwing, mistle thrush, long-tailed tit, goldcrest, wren, woodcock, snipe and water rail. A bittern and two choughs were also picked up dead. The cruellest moment came in mid-January when a thaw and rain by day were followed by a sudden hard frost at night and birds woke next morning to find themselves frozen to their perches both on the ground and in trees and bushes, and many were held by the ice until they died.

That was the winter which robbed us of our favourite song-bird. Till then the woodlark was in good numbers here, singing almost the year round, even in winter if the day was mild. My diary chronicles its singing in the Indian summer of 1962. On September 29 the morning was blue and still as the tide came up the estuary. A woodlark sang by the pines as I passed by and even when I was right out on the salt-marshes I could still hear his far-carrying song along with the *tew-tew-tew* of greenshanks and the whistling of newly arrived wigeon. The lovely weather went on and so did the singing of the woodlark. On October 5 I noted: 'Heavenly song all this still sunny morning'. And on October 13: 'Our woodlark sings by the house for hours most mornings in this lovely halcyon weather'. But before the end of October the anticyclone drifted away and cold rain brought an end to all woodlark rhapsodies. Then came December and the Siberian weather and in the spring that followed we listened in vain for our woodlarks. In the ordinary run of events, after every awesome winter, there are these sad losses but then Mother Nature sets about stitching the world together again and in two or three years even the most decimated birds recover their numbers. But this did not happen to the woodlark. Even now, over thirty years later, we still have no woodlarks.

By coincidence the loss of one bird from this district was quickly followed by the arrival of another, though the newcomer was a poor substitute for the woodlark. When spring came in 1963 I went off down the coast in the hope of seeing the latest addition to Cardiganshire's birds. Little did I think when I managed to spot my first collared dove (it was in the leafy grounds of Cardigan Castle) that in only two or three years these doves would be accepted as familiar garden birds in many of our local towns and villages. Not that they have yet settled in our garden at Ynys Edwin even now. We hear their notes every spring from nearby trees but then they move on like passing migrants. Evidently we are in too wild a spot for their particular life-style.

Chapter 9

In spring, 1963, James Fisher, then a presenter of radio nature programmes at Bristol, gave £25 of the BBC's money to each of three birdwatchers of long experience to be spent by them in searching for a wild bird they had never seen before. The rules imposed were simple. 'Here's £25. Go and look for your bird. All expenditure demanded by the search must come out of the £25. No more is to be spent except in the direst emergency. The bird sought for must be declared in advance.' Elizabeth Forster of Norfolk chose to go to France to try for a flamingo. Denzil Harber from Sussex would go to Denmark for a thrush-nightingale. My choice was the black woodpecker mainly because it looked so spectacular in the bird books—the size of a crow, all-black except for a bright-red top to his head and with a beak that was said to be capable of hacking chips nine inches long out of trees. But I took a risk in electing to go to a district in France which was right on the edge of the black woodpecker's range (it has spread westwards since then). There was also the fact that all woodpeckers, even where common, can be extremely elusive.

I drove across Wales, England and France to near Dijon, a journey that cost me much of the £25. But I had no other expenses. I took all my food from home and, to avoid overnight fees, I camped each night in roadside woods and disused quarries. Although this avoidance of official camp-sites had its hazards there was only one spot where I almost got into difficulties. I had driven at dusk along a track into a forest and was awakened early next morning by a gamekeeper who was clearly not pleased to find me and my car deep in his coverts. I did my halting best to explain to him that I was '*un observateur des oiseaux*' and not a poacher after his pheasants. This mention of pheasants proved fortunate. It changed the whole atmosphere. The keeper seemed to find the idea of his being a guardian of pheasants quite amusing. His reserve, he assured me with some pride, was for the hunting of wild boar and roe deer. After that he became really affable and told me about some of the birds of the forest and how '*le *milan royal* (red kite) and '*l'autour*' (goshawk) were getting scarcer year by year. Then off he went through the trees, leaving me to have my breakfast in peace, if I can speak of peace when ten thousand frogs were shouting themselves hoarse in a nearby swamp.

I explored that countryside for several days—a gently beautiful land with pinewoods on the hills and wide cornlands between. The wildflowers were spectacular, especially the orchids: long stretches of the lanesides had lady and military orchids in full bloom. Along the forest edges there were crested tits and often the stuttering little songs of Bonelli's warblers. All week the weather was perfect for sleeping out and I never unpacked my tent. But the absence of black woodpeckers was worrying and I was beginning to wonder whether to make a quick dash to the Vosges Mountains or perhaps the Jura.

But I decided to stay where I was. Then on almost my last morning I lay listening to the dawn chorus in a woodland of beech and pine. I could hear hoopoes, quails (in the field outside), cuckoos, blackcaps, orioles and blackbirds imitating orioles rather well. It is a magical moment when you wake up in a strange forest and have no idea what you may hear or see next. That dawn, as I lay there, I heard a startling noise high in the trees: *kok-kok-kok-keear*. Then I saw the bird which had produced it, looking very large and black as it came flapping over my clearing a few yards above my face. That was how the black woodpecker came into my life. I lay a few minutes listening but he didn't come back. Then I heard a loud *klonk-klonk* of beak on hard wood about a hundred yards off. So I got out of my bag and went through the trees as quietly as I could. Soon I saw him, high up a pine, the great black woodpecker with his scarlet crown, banging away at a dead branch. I watched him for several minutes. Then he saw me and away he went, not undulating like the smaller woodpeckers, but flying almost floppily like a jay. And that was how the black woodpecker went out of my life, for I have never seen another.

I was leaving the Dijon country and heading for home when a road-sign caught my eye. It pointed over a stream and up a lane and said 'St Germain—Source-Seine 4'. How could I resist visiting the well-spring of so famous a river? Would the Seine, I wondered, come trickling out of a mountain flank like the Wye in Wales? I drove across a gently rolling limestone plateau through unfenced patches of

147

light woodland—pine, beech, hornbeam, whitebeam, oak, wych elm and erect bushes of juniper—which were separated by stretches of wild open country. There were few signs of human occupation; and flowers were everywhere—white rockrose, hoary plantain, twin-flowered honeysuckle, cowslips, goldilocks buttercup, round-headed rampion, Watling Street thistle, green-winged orchids, lady orchids, military orchids; and butterflies everywhere: brimstones, orange-tips, wood whites and various unidentified skippers and fritillaries. Scarce swallowtails glided and swooped spectacularly.

Birds sang all round—skylarks, woodlarks, tree pipits, whinchats, serins, orioles and many others. And as I lay by the infant Seine that night I could hardly sleep for nightingales and the unending *ke-oo* of Scops owls. But I was disappointed by the source of the Seine. It had long ago been acquired by the City of Paris and made to flow from an

The so-called scarce swallowtail was not uncommon at the source of the Seine, May 1963.

The grotto at the source of the River Seine in eastern France built by the City of Paris in 1865.

artificial grotto. A statue of the river goddess, Sequana, stood behind iron railings and there was a souvenir shop not far away. It was the old, old story—vulgarisation for the sake of tourism. All the same I was lucky it was springtime, for a local man I spoke to told me that summer up there can sometimes be very hot and dusty and the infant Seine may run completely dry for miles. So give me the Welsh Wye and the Welsh rain any day! From the source of the Seine I had to hurry back to the BBC studios at Bristol to report on my black woodpecker. In the programme we also heard Elizabeth Forster bubbling over about the pink cloud of flamingos she had seen across the lagunas of the Camargue; and in Denmark Denzil Harber had been equally successful in getting his first thrush-nightingale.

That spring was destined to be a season of rare birds. I was hardly back from my black woodpecker adventure when the 'phone rang to report the latest excitement: the vicar, R. S. Thomas, had found a nest of Montagu's harriers in one of our local reed beds. The discovery was momentous because although this harrier had long nested very sparingly in the coastal counties of Wales it had never been known to breed in our district and certainly not in our parish. So passed a memorable season. With these rare and beautiful hawks breeding less than a mile away we quite frequently saw them rolling past close to the ground on graceful, long-winged, buoyant flight, sometimes the almost white male, sometimes the dark-brown female. Then in August, after a successful breeding season, the harriers left us for their wintering grounds in Africa. They have never come back. Probably while on migration they met with disaster. And where more likely than in some Mediterranean locality where migrant harriers are regularly shot for target practice by what pass for sportsmen in that uncivilised region. About that time Montagu's harriers ceased to nest anywhere in Wales. I know that every generation of naturalists has reason to lament over departed glories. On my list the loss of Montagu's harrier ranks high.

That year of rare birds also brought a rare plant. In September I was crossing a ridge in Snowdonia, keeping my eyes open for alpines, when I happened to glance at a wayside boulder and saw a line of little ferns growing out of a horizontal crack. There was something about those ferns that made me stoop to examine them though they were less than two inches in length of frond. Though I could not put a name to these fernlets I knew enough about the common small ferns of mountains to realise that I was faced with something new. The nearest I could think of was the brittle bladder fern: but that is a smooth, shiny, hairless fern whereas this new find was rather matt, not so bright-green and distinctly hairy. When I got home and looked it up in a flora I realised I had stumbled on what was apparently a new locality for that rarity, the oblong woodsia.

This discovery turned me overnight into a woodsia enthusiast and I have since been back to Snowdonia many times looking for this little fern and its close cousin, the alpine woodsia, but both are desperately hard to find. In the seventeenth century Edward Lhuyd noted them

Male redstart at a nest-box on a bedroom window ledge at Ynys Edwin.

Woodlark nesting in a field at Ynys-hir, 1960.

Clogwyn Du'r Arddu, one of the cliffs of Snowdon.

as rare even then. So after the nineteenth century's fern-collecting mania and the twentieth century's special contribution of acid rain, it is quite wonderful that any woodsias survive. Yet after thirty years the oblong woodsia still thrives on the boulder where I first found it and in precisely the same crack. Sheep occasionally nibble at it but do not destroy it.

Years after this find I was able to go to the Natural History Museum in London where the fern expert, Clive Jermy, kindly showed me their large collection of woodsias from Britain and around the world. It was wonderful to see them but depressing to think that, as far as Britain is concerned, there must be far more dead woodsias in this and other collections than there are living in the wild. What was striking was the size of some of the fronds from abroad—four or five times longer than Snowdonia's woodsias. It left me with a yearning to see the oblong woodsia in the White Mountains of New Hampshire where it is said to grow quite commonly on screes, as parsley fern does in Britain, and to reach ten inches long. Most moving of all in the British Museum was to be shown the actual specimens of woodsia collected on Snowdon by Edward Lhuyd three hundred years ago and still labelled in his handwriting.

★   ★   ★

In October, 1963, Penny and I made the only long break in our life in Wales. It came about through Mary Richards. For years we had enjoyed her frequent companionship, botanising and birdwatching in Wales. But in 1950 she had gone off for a long holiday at the invitation of old friends in Northern Rhodesia (now Zambia). There, aged 65, she had fallen deeply in love with Africa. After that she became an annual visitor to Abercorn (now Mbala) where her friends had their estate and eventually she got a home of her own there, an isolated place five miles into the loneliness of the bush. By then, transferring her botanical allegiences from Wales to Africa, she had become a zestful plant collector, sending countless sheets of meticulously pressed plants to Kew Herbarium and other collections. Many were new to science and several are named in her honour.

She wrote us letter after letter about the wondrous wildlife out there—the plants, trees, mammals, birds, butterflies—especially

151

those to be seen on the wild, grassy Rukwa Plain on the hot floor of the western arm of the Great Rift Valley. She continually urged us to go and see these delights. But, we asked ourselves, where were we to find the fare? Around that time I had to go to London to see Collins the publishers in connection with the New Naturalist book they had asked me to write about Snowdonia. I was introduced to the head of the firm, the late Billy Collins, and in the course of conversation I light-heartedly suggested that he might advance enough money to get Penny and me to Africa and back so that in return I could write a book about birdwatching there. To my astonishment he agreed on the spot.

So off we went, innocents going abroad, knowing absolutely nothing about Africa and very nervous about how we would stand up to the climate of the Great Rift Valley. Certainly something we had not anticipated was the drama of Africa's fluctuating water levels. We had been hearing for years about this vast and beautiful Rukwa Plain, yet by the time we got there Mother Nature had waved her wand and had transformed it into the vast and beautiful Rukwa Lake. Only then did we learn about Rukwa's strange history and how, two or three times a century, it changed from a plain to a lake then back again to a plain. In both halves of its cycle it has always been rich in wildlife: as a plain it is a home for zebras, giraffes, elephants, buffaloes, impala, reed-bucks, topi and other antelopes as well as countless birds; as a lake it has a multitude of fish, crocodiles, hippos, along with pelicans and other aquatic fowl in huge numbers. When we first saw the lake in October, 1963, it stretched for seventy miles and was still spreading. And I'm told it is still a lake today, the Rukwa region having escaped the droughts which have lately affected neighbouring parts of Africa.

We were with Mary Richards for five months, much of the time on trips to some of her favourite playgrounds, not only the Rukwa Valley but also Lake Tanganyika; the hills, woods and gorges around Abercorn; and the Southern Highlands of what is now Tanzania. Mary had an insatiable love of camping and we spent much of our time under canvas in completely wild country far from the tourist routes. She despised national parks: they were too tame, too organised and too well known botanically. She wanted the true wilderness, the

152

botanically unexplored, the really adventurous. She laughingly prided herself on being a Victorian (she was born in 1885) and her heroines were the redoubtable lady explorers and travellers of the nineteenth century.

When the time came for us to leave we had learned to love Africa. We had survived the horrendous heat, the deeply pot-holed, often flooded tracks, the mosquitos and the tsetse flies of the Great Rift Valley. We had even found frost on the mountains and had felt cold in our beds. We had seen countless wonders—plants, trees, birds,

Black-winged kite, Zambia, February 1964.

153

A well-camouflaged two-banded courser on a plain in Tanzania.

mammals, brilliant butterflies, splendid hawkmoths, caterpillars of outlandish size, colourful lizards, praying mantises, carpets of dragonflies, huge flying grasshoppers we mistook for birds. We had enjoyed the frequent company of one of the finest all-round naturalists then in Africa, Desmond Vesey-FitzGerald. We had made friends among African people, witnessed their transition from white rule to independence and hoped that their future would be better than their past. It was a grey, cold first of March when we got back home to Wales and quite abruptly our African experience seemed very far away.

★   ★   ★

It is always a happiness for botanists to find a rare plant in a new locality. The next best thing is to rediscover a long-lost one, as a group of us managed to do on June 20, 1964, while on an outing of the West Wales Field Society in Merioneth. From Trawsfynydd we went east up Cwm Prysor, botanising along the recently abandoned railway. Eventually we came to a small pallid cliff which we didn't need to be geologists to recognise as an outcrop of limestone, for it was patched yellow with rockrose, a truly rare plant in that part of Wales. With it we found shining cranesbill, Forster's stonecrop, brittle bladder fern, burnet saxifrage, marjoram and a few lime-loving mosses and liverworts. But the best find of the day was northern bedstraw (*Galium boreale*) which had been reported many years before from Cwm Prysor but not seen since.

Its original discoverer on that hill was one of the best-known north Wales naturalists of his day, Thomas Ruddy, head gardener of the Palé estate near Llangollen. A man of wide interests, Ruddy was popular as a leader of field excursions and as a contributor of nature notes to newspapers and journals. Much of what he wrote is still available in reference libraries in that treasure-house of local knowledge, *Bye-gones*. I regret I never met Thomas Ruddy who came all the way from Llangollen and found the northern bedstraw in Cwm Prysor.

★   ★   ★

One day Hubert Mappin lent me a book that turned my thoughts westwards across the sea. I had long felt drawn to visit the land of my ancestors and Praeger's *A Botanist in Ireland* made it clear that such a visit must not be put off any longer. The message we got from Praeger was that wherever we might go in Ireland the wildflowers would give a lift to our spirits but that the truly marvellous place to see was the region of limestone hills, wild and largely unpeopled, called the Burren that looks across the sea over in the west in County Clare.

So one spring day to the Burren we went with our friends Cecil and Jonny Lambourne and rejoiced in vast spreads of mountain avens which blended perfectly with a wondrous opulence of bloody

155

cranesbill, hoary rockrose and early purple orchids. Here and there we found ourselves walking through intensely blue swards of spring gentian. There were flowers everywhere—birdsfoot trefoil, ox-eye daisy, thyme, yellow-wort, scurvy-grass, mountain everlasting, vernal sandwort and many others, all in abundance. We clambered up tilted sheets of gleaming white rock to reach plant-rich ledges. We peeped into deep crevices where in shade and moistness grew healthy forests of hartstongue and maidenhair ferns. From hill tops we saw the pale shapes of the three Aran Islands out in the isolation of the western sea. In the north we looked far away to the beckoning Twelve Bens of Connemara. Lately we have heard with total loathing of a proposal thought up by insensitive politicians, entrepreneurs or tourism promoters (they're all the same really—none of them can see further than the nearest money-bags). Their idea is to exploit this miraculously surviving Burren by establishing a huge visitor centre there. Inevitably, there is strong opposition to this scheme and so far the matter is unresolved but conservationists pray that the whole Burren flora will be given the full protection it so outstandingly deserves.

Home from our safari in Ireland, I was soon deep into a survey of heronries for a list of the birds of Cardiganshire which the West Wales Field Society was about to publish. Its chief authors were Geoffrey Ingram and Col Morrey Salmon, both of Cardiff, and as neither had done much recent bird-watching in Cardiganshire they had asked me to bring the records up to date. For decades Ingram and Salmon were the inseparable leading lights in south Wales ornithology. In fact so many notes appeared in the literature over the names of Ingram and Salmon that eventually *Punch* magazine decided they must be one person and duly printed their name as 'Ingramandsalmon'. Their close relationship never waned. When Ingram declined into feeble old age, Salmon made a point of going round to spend an evening with him once a week for several years until the end.

It was said of Morrey Salmon that, apart from his family, he had three great loves of his life: the Welch Regiment, the National Museum of Wales and the red kite. To all three he gave distinguished voluntary service of long duration. He was small, slim, upright and keen-eyed into extreme old age. He kept himself fit and even when he fell out of an apple tree at the age of ninety he suffered no ill effects. Few have worked harder or longer for the conservation of natural habitats. That the flowery dunes and bird-rich lake at Kenfig near Swansea, for instance, are now a nature reserve, owes much to his dogged persistence. That was only one of many choice spots for which he did battle against the philistines.

His researches into the annals of the red kite in Wales this century were immense. Ask him about a record of any kite's nest in any year and he could usually give you details of its success or failure. He knew nearly everyone who had ever had a hand in kite protection since it began in 1903; and he kept a file on all egg-collectors too. His knowledge of British birds was encyclopaedic and he had endless stories of the early days of bird-photography, usually in the company of Geoffrey Ingram; or with Arthur Brook of Aberedw whom he described as 'the outstanding bird-photographer of his generation', a generous tribute from one who had himself done so much to pioneer bird-photography.

Taking stock of Cardiganshire's heronries proved a delightful exercise. Most of the heronries were in beautiful sites, often along rivers and on old private estates where possibly they dated back centuries. So I found myself visiting genteel homes and interviewing their few surviving genteel owners, all of them helpful and welcoming. There was clearly a strong desire that the heronries should be safeguarded, a sentiment that was probably a throw-back to long-held traditions that should an estate's heronry come to an end, so would the estate's family. It seems that it was back in the Middle Ages that heronries and private estates became inextricably linked. The herons were encouraged to nest near mansions because they were popular as a quarry for falcons. Besides, young herons were also good to eat. In my 1965 census I could find only six heronries, their total of nests being forty-four, a figure probably well below average because many herons were believed to have perished in the winter of 1962-3.

Frost was on our minds in that spring of 1965. When I was a child my father used to speak in awed tones of 'the great May snowstorm'. I have no idea what that year was but it was clearly an event that stayed large in his mind. Similarly I retain a memory, not of a great May snowstorm but of a great May frost. We are all used to the early spring frosts that strike so gleefully at gardens, orchards and early potato fields. But the May frost of 1965 was a worse stab in the back than most because it struck at us in the third week of the month, by which time here in the west we have normally stopped worrying about serious frost. The night of May 22 brought total ruin to potatoes, runner beans and other garden tenderlings. But it was out in the countryside that the effects were most startling. Never before had we seen lowland woods of oak and ash blasted in full leaf and turned completely black. And black they remained until they found the heart to put out new greenery late in June.

The year of the great May frost, was also the year of the great December flood. The Cambrian Mountains, from Arennig to Plynlimon, had mothered a prodigious amount of rain, and Severn, Wye, Dee, Dyfi, Mawddach and most other mid-Wales rivers burst hugely over their banks twice in a week. On December 12 I was in the Midlands motoring back to Wales. I came via Kidderminster intending to cross the Severn at Bewdley but the approaches to the bridge were several feet under water. I hesitated whether to turn upstream or downstream and decided to go down to Stourport. There the scene was the same—the surging brown flood with the road to the bridge under water. Holt Fleet bridge was even more unapproachable, for the land along the Severn just there is very low-lying. And of course, Worcester, notorious for going under water by the bridge and the county cricket ground, was out of the question. I finally crossed the river on the high new bridge at Tewkesbury, having added hugely to the length of my journey. But in retrospect it was worth it to see that majestic flood rolling down the valley of the middle Severn because it had rained the day before on Plynlimon.

*   *   *

In the following spring R. S. Thomas and I exchanged the moist green hills of Wales for what, in all but name, was a piece of the Sahara. We had been drawn to the Coto Doñana, near Seville, by Guy Mountfort's *Portrait of a Wilderness* which had described irresistibly this wildlife-rich region of estuary marshes, cork-oak woods and far-spreading, mountainous sand dunes. Mountfort, we

Caterpillar of the bedstraw hawkmoth in the Coto Doñana near Seville, May 1966. Colour pale-green with nine black-edged yellow spots and a crimson horn.

found, had not exaggerated. The marshes were lively with pratincoles, stilts, squacco herons, night herons and various terns. Mixed colonies of grey herons, cattle egrets, little egrets, spoonbills and storks crowded some of the trees with their nests. Flamingos were distant passing pink clouds. Kites, both black and red, circled overhead, ready to dive and snatch at anything edible. Far away above the woodlands we saw a magnificent pair of imperial eagles. Great spotted cuckoos chattered everywhere in the thickets; and we never got used to the colourfulness of hoopoes, rollers, orioles, bee-eaters and azure-winged magpies. Unfamiliar warblers sang from every bush; and the tiny fan-tailed cisticola, lisping his feeble notes high in the air, was a real touch of Africa.

From the heat and mosquitos of the Coto Doñana we made for the heights of Ronda, a high range of limestone mountains broken by spectacular cliffs and gorges. In cool upland breezes we saw choughs, vultures, lesser kestrels, Bonelli's eagles, rock buntings, rock sparrows, black wheatears, great grey shrikes, red-rumped swallows and alpine swifts. I won't even begin on the wonderfully varied and colourful wildflowers, especially the orchids. On our way back across Spain we saw snakes, scorpions, mole-crickets and butterflies that were new to us. A final memory, as we came back over the snow-capped Pyrenees through Andorra, is of alpine accentors, blue rock thrushes and water pipits on wild slopes coloured with narcissi, crocuses, gentians and anemones.

★   ★   ★

There was an unusual event a few months later: I was able to add a new native tree to my life list, a tree that someone had spotted less than three miles from where I live. It was a wild service (*Sorbus torminalis*). When I went off with R. S. Thomas to see this rarity we found there were in fact seven trees in all, in a close group on the side of a rocky dingle amongst old oaks. Three were mature and had clusters of brown berries, the rest being very young. They were all so near to each other they could well have been growing from one root. We were left wondering whether they were a relict of a time when perhaps service trees were more widespread in this part of Wales. If so, it was probably long ago because its Welsh name, *cerddinen wyllt*, seems to be unknown hereabouts.

In that same year (1966) I was indirectly involved in the finding of another rarity. I had just written a book about the Snowdonia National Park and in it I mentioned spignel (*Meum athamanticum*), a fennel-like meadow plant, sometimes used medicinally, that is widespread on some of the uplands of Europe, including Scotland, but is very uncommon in Wales. It had been reported three centuries ago by Edward Lhuyd who said he found it near Llanuwchllyn, south-west of Bala, and that the locality was actually known as Bryn y Ffenigl, a name which, according to dictionaries, can mean either 'fennel hill' or 'spignel hill'. I admitted in my book that I had failed to find this locality but suggested that some keen researcher might be able to bring it to light. The book had not been out many months when I got a letter from a reader who, while on holiday at Llanuwchllyn, had not only located Bryn y Ffenigl but had even found spignel still plentiful there. If this really was the first record of spignel in that locality since Lhuyd's day (and I believe it may have been) then this surely must be a record time for a plant to have been lost and then refound?

★   ★   ★

For many joyful years we were privileged to have in our parish an artist of distinction, Mildred E. Eldrige (Elsi to her friends), wife of the poet-vicar, R. S. Thomas. We treasure the memory not only of her beautiful landscapes and her meticulous studies of birds, butterflies, moths and plants but also for the fine mural she painted for the nurses' dining-room at the orthopaedic hospital at Gobowen. We first saw it in its early stages in the vicarage at Manafon, Montgomeryshire. Then, when R. S. Thomas became vicar here at Eglwys-fach, we met with it again, still as a work in progress, fixed temporarily round the walls of the vicarage dining-room. Its theme was of an allegorical nature but the margins were illuminated as in a medieval manuscript by exquisite images of miscellaneous natural objects. Elsi encouraged us to bring her anything we found of interest. So we got into the habit of taking her a shell, a feather, a butterfly's wing or a wildflower or maybe some poor dead chaffinch we had picked up on the road. Next time we called, there they would be, painted with wonderful delicacy along the border of her mural.

One day in the vicarage garden we found a swift which had evidently come from one of the nests under the eaves and had grounded itself, though for no obvious reason. We always envied the vicarage for its colony of swifts. If only we could have swifts nesting at Ynys Edwin, we thought. And one year it looked as if we might. High up in our south-facing wall there used to be a hole where a stone had fallen out. It had been a home for sparrows but when, with our arrival, the house ceased to be a farmhouse, the sparrows departed for ever, no doubt disgusted at seeing the farmyard tidied up, the poultry gone and with them large supplies of food. Then in our ninth summer here, in mid-June, we were amazed to see a pair of swifts showing an interest in that hole, persistently swooping up to it then falling away, just like fulmars prospecting for nest-sites on a sea cliff. For four days they dropped in to see us twice daily as part of their social round. Then their visits grew less regular and ceased altogether after the first of July. That they have never come back does not surprise us. Swifts are conservative and their numbers must be very stable, for they remain faithful to old nesting places and seldom seem to colonise new ones. When we first came to this parish the strongest swift colony was even then under the eaves of the vicarage. Over forty years later the swifts remain. It is the vicars who have flown.

*   *   *

In July, 1967, a change of scene. My birding friend Francis Peach took me on a tour of East African game parks. He had inherited a little cash from his father and, as he put it: 'Pop wouldn't have imagined a better use of this money than that you and I should spend it on a wildlife trip'. So Francis bought a package tour which took us on a conventional round of reserves from Nairobi: Tsavo, Ngorongoro Crater, Serengeti, Olduvai Gorge, Masai Mara, Hell's Gate, Lake Naivasha, Tree Tops, the Kenya Safari Club, Lake Nakuru and Nairobi National Park.

From Nairobi we travelled by tarmac roads, then bumpy trackways, in a minibus painted with zebra stripes, our companions two middle-aged American couples from the Middle West. So for an extraordinary fortnight we forgot about the urbanised world and went out into the arid plains and the acacia savannas scattered with palms and ancient baobabs, to share life with buffaloes, warthogs, jackals, hyenas, wild dogs, wildebeests, zebras, hippos and bat-eared foxes. We stood under an acacia while a leopard dozed on a branch above. We passed within a few yards of a family of cheetahs which ignored us aloofly. We looked up at giraffes and down at duikers. We stopped respectfully while elephants and elephant children crossed the trail ahead. Sadly we interviewed, from a safe distance, what could be an animal on its way out of the world—the rhinoceros. At Nakuru we stood amazed by a lake pink with a quarter of a million flamingos. (Numbers were 'well down' that year we were told.)

As Francis and I were keen to list the birds as well as the mammals we soon got tired of being taken from one pride of lions to another. 'Birds', we said to our African driver, 'we'd like to see birds'. He looked blank until we got the word *endegi* out of a Swahili phrase-book. Then his face lit up and away we went in search of *endegi*. A mile along the road we stopped and our driver pointed in triumph to a magnificent tawny eagle on top of a telephone pole. A good start, we thought. But what we didn't know was that a great many roadside

162

Cheetahs often ignored vehicles driving past them on the plains of Serengeti, July 1967.

poles in that part of Africa have a magnificent tawny eagle perched atop of them. It took us a long time before we got it across to our driver that we had no desire to stop at every tawny eagle and that there were other birds in the world.

Our hope had been to see about 250 kinds of birds but having frittered so many precious hours pursuing those boring lions (many wearing the off-putting coloured ear-tags of scientific research) we finished with a bird score of only 206. Many have remained very bright in my memory. The white-headed buffalo weaver that shows a scarlet rump as it flies; the huge pale Kori bustards walking gravely away through the tall grasses rather than flying; another long-shanked walker, the secretary bird, striding with dignity across the plain; lammergeyers and Ruppell's griffons magnificent in the upper airs; a majestic black-chested harrier eagle on a dead tree-top at dawn; and in a butterfly-rich forest close to Nairobi two wonderful bird voices—the indescribable harsh barking of Hartlaub's turaco and that gentlest, most apologetic of all sounds, the cooing of Narina's trogon.

We had experienced, however briefly, a fragment of the world's greatest rift valley, a trench still haunted by the volcanoes and earthquakes that attended its creation. We had looked along infinite miles of escarpment walls with their baked and naked cliffs. We had seen tawny, sunburnt plains scattered with soda lakes, some clear and shining, some darkly blue-green and sinister. We had descended into Africa's hugest caldera and climbed out of it ten miles away on the opposite side. We had passed through the throat of a ravine under towering, vulture-haunted buttresses. Yet never did we really grasp the vastness and the meaning of that harsh and crumpled landscape which stretched between us and those dormant or dead volcanoes whose peaks stood solitary along far-away horizons.

As our homeward-bound aircraft rose above the outskirts of Nairobi, Francis came out with one of those statistics I can never remember accurately but it was to the effect that every time a big jet plane gets airborne it uses, in those first thunderous five minutes of up-thrust, as much fuel as an average car burns in five or six years. Ours was not a huge plane yet we must have made a fair contribution to atmospheric damage and waste of fossil fuels in our several hours of flying back to London. So though our minds ought to have been radiant with the after-glow of the East African sunshine, we got into a mournful conversation about the evils of tourism. But we could also see that without the planes to bring in the tourists there would not be any of those wonderful African parks. So, thirty thousand feet above Mother Earth, we debated green issues but I don't remember that we reached any useful conclusions.

Chapter 10

Kingfishers and martins, nesting in river banks, must live lives of quiet desperation when rains are heavy and waters rise. But the risks they run are nothing compared with those faced by birds that nest along estuaries, for they are at the mercy of the tides that come up the rivers as well as the floods that come down them. Bordering our estuary of the Dyfi there are many acres of rushes and grassland which to larks, pipits, reed buntings, lapwings and redshanks must look like God's gift to ground-nesting birds. But what these birds have never learnt is that every fortnight, at full moon and new moon, the tides rise high; and if there is anything more than a light wind from the west, or if an extra spate is coming down from the mountains, then the waters may cover the whole estuary floodplain and swamp every nest.

On April 26, 1969, walking across the estuary saltings, I happened to disturb a redshank off a nest deep in a grassy tussock. It was a period of calm weather and all went well with that nest until May 4. That night a wind sprang out of the west and the full-moon tide rose just high enough to cover the redshank's nest though perhaps by only an inch of water. When I looked next morning the four eggs were still in place, but were stone cold. Yet that same night a nearby meadow pipit's nest, placed a little higher in its tussock than the redshank's nest, had just managed to escape. We can picture the little bird incubating her eggs as the water spreads everywhere just an inch or two below her in the darkness yet does not quite reach her. Next day's tides are less and the brood is eventually reared successfully. Such are the dramas of estuary life.

★   ★   ★

That spring Penny and I went north to visit some of Scotland's more famous reserves with our old friends Cecil and Jonny Lambourne of Worcestershire; and we came home with our minds full of bright images that have never faded. Among the veteran pines of Rothiemurchus and elsewhere, a few especially ancient trees of vast girth and perfect dignity; slender junipers, tall and erect among the pines; chickweed wintergreen and lesser twayblade giving a touch of variety to moss-floored woodlands. We went right up to the wild north coast and lived a few days at the foot of two shapely peaks —Ben Hope and Ben Loyal. Golden eagles and hen harriers over the moors; red-necked phalaropes swimming tamely at a lake-edge; red-throated divers coming inland from off the sea at dawn and vanishing into the hills; the tiny jewel called Scottish primrose everywhere in

We found the Scottish primrose plentiful along the Sutherland coast in May 1969. It is now reported to be in serious decline.

'Dr. Johnson's rock-cresse' now called northern rockcress (*Cardaminopsis petraea*) on Clogwyn Du'r Arddu, Snowdon.

Leopard, Serengeti, Tanzania.

Eastern bluebird. *(Courtesy of Karl Schanz)*

the coastal turf; twites perched in rows along the wires. Sheets of mountain avens, bearberry and purple mountain milk-vetch in the dunes at Bettyhill.

We moved south to the uplands of Inchnadamph where there were lime-rich and lime-less tracts of country side by side, each with plants quite new to our southern eyes. Never had we dreamt that there was so much holly fern anywhere in the world. Here too a twelve-inch-high forest of the beautiful myrtle-leaved willow. Next came the woods, moors and mountains of the huge reserve at Inverpolly, as perfect a stretch of near wilderness as you will find anywhere in Britain. Then we were on the banks of Loch Maree with its fine oakwoods along the farther shore; and redwings singing in its alder groves. We scrambled far up the slopes of Beinn Eighe looking for pine martens but in vain. We came to the pathetic remains of Britain's most northerly ashwood at Rassal and saw how it was being saved at the eleventh hour. We came home full of the grandeur of Scotland's high rugged mountains. But we were even more impressed by the hugeness of the glens compared with the valleys of Wales. Crows can speak to each other easily across almost any valley in Wales; but across the bigger Scottish glens they would need loud-hailers.

A bird we had confidently expected to hear in north-west Scotland was the corncrake; but though we were told exactly where to go, no corncrake craked for us. Yet we hadn't been home from Scotland very long when a local farmer 'phoned to say that his mowing machine had destroyed a corncrake's nest. He would not have noticed it if the nest had not been built into a large tussock of grass which had stopped the cutter. I went to see. Eight red-spotted buff eggs were scattered about, half of them smashed. So calamity had struck what was probably the very last nest in this neighbourhood of the poor, inoffensive corncrake, an elusive, brownish, ground-running bird no bigger than a starling but with a voice as loud as a crow's.

Long centuries ago farming created a perfect world for corncrakes by clearing the forests to make hayfields (corncrakes were never birds of the corn); and the *crek-crek* mating call, heard all night as well as all day, was well known to most country people. But our century's style of farming has brought disaster by the mechanisation of hay-cutting and by the development of earlier maturing types of grass which meant that hay was cut just when corncrakes were incubating their eggs. I have on my shelves a rural encyclopaedia of 1845. Read what it says about corncrakes and live for a moment in another age: 'The corncrake is exceedingly abundant in some places. It begins to be heard in the British Isles about the middle of May. It continues its peculiar cry during all the breeding season. It breeds on the ground and makes its nest of dry moss and dry grass. Its young run as soon as they leave the nest and become able in six weeks to fly but seldom quit the meadow till the scythe lays bare their habitation'.

*   *   *

Let me recall a hawkmoth incident. In August 1969, there were unprecedented numbers of eyed hawkmoth caterpillars on the sallow leaves. It must have been one of those years when their dreaded enemies, the ichneumon flies, were either scarce or had found other victims. I brought one of these caterpillars home. It was large, chubby and yellow-green and had seven white stripes slanting down each side. There was a curved spike on its tail-end—the hallmark of most hawkmoth caterpillars. I put it in a box of sand and in a day or two it had dug down and disappeared to pupate.

Out of that sand the following June, crawled a perfect female eyed hawkmoth. (Can we ever hope to understand the chemistry of such a miraculous metamorphosis?) Just before midnight I took her outside, opened the box and waited for her to vibrate her wings with ever increasing speed, then roar off into the darkness, as I have seen so many moths do. Nothing of the sort happened. Instead a male moth came flying in out of the night and immediately mated with her in the box. What subtle, far-carrying messages insects have for each other!

That year, in June, I saw a hawkmoth I have seldom met with—the small elephant. I was on the track up our local hill, Foel Fawr, and there was this exquisite creature, a wonder of delicate shades of pink and green, lying in bright sunlight on a mat of its sweetly-scented, white-flowered food plant, heath bedstraw. That was also a puss-moth year. Their grotesque larvae, large, bright-green and purple,

168

hump-backed, flat-faced, tail-lashing and juice-squirting, were in dozens on the sallows and were at all stages of growth from newly hatched to fully developed. Never again have I seen puss-moth caterpillars anything like so abundant.

*   *   *

For several years in the 1960s we used to get a 'phone-call about the end of June from our friend Norman Hunter of Machynlleth, giving us his annual bee orchid count from the sand dunes at Aberdyfi, one of the very few localities in mid-Wales for an orchid that is best known in chalk or limestone districts. Bee orchid numbers fluctuate wildly from year to year. Sometimes Norman's score was near to zero, in other years it might be over a hundred. It was through playing golf that Norman became aware of Aberdyfi's bee orchids because they happen to grow where the sand dunes and the golf course merge into each other. He knew all the right spots and as he went from green to green he kept a tally of the orchids as well as of his golf score.

We remember Norman not only as a counter of bee orchids (he never reported his golf scores) but also for his writings. As N. C. Hunter the dramatist, hailed in the 1950s as an English Chekhov, he wrote those delightfully civilised plays *The Waters of the Moon, A Day by the Sea, A Touch of the Sun* and *The Tulip Tree.* He was a gentle, dear man who loved rural Wales, trees, mountains, his garden, butterflies, moths and bee orchids. I am almost forgetting the autumn lady's tresses which also grow round the golf course. These he counted for us every year in September.

I should spare a thought for another local man, George Paddock, before he is completely forgotten. He was the owner of this estate of Ynys-hir a century ago and from all accounts was a man of energy. It seems to have been Paddock who planted many of the specimen trees that still adorn Ynys-hir and probably it was he who ordered the building of many of the walls which still enclose the oakwoods. Certainly he made the long, low, stone defence that curves out into the estuary along the western edge of the property. It was aimed to turn an area of mud into a large acreage of saltmarsh pasture and in this it succeeded. Sheep in their hundreds now graze there on healthy ground free from liver fluke which does not thrive in salty conditions.

This stone wall is marked prosaically on the map as 'Breakwater'. But in the days of its making and for long afterwards it was known as 'Paddock's Pier'. When it was being built it was a godsend to the many tramps who used to pass along the Machynlleth-Aberystwyth road, for they could always earn a little money helping to build Paddock's Pier. This name has long ago faded from local speech and as far as I know there is only one other besides myself who remembers it. And since neither of us are in our first youth it cannot be long before the name passes into complete oblivion. By then Paddock will be remembered hereabouts only by his ivied gravestone under a yew tree in our village churchyard: 'In memory of George Paddock JP, DL, of Barlaston, Staffordshire and Ynys-Hir, Glandovey. Born 1st April, 1822. Died 16th April, 1895'.

*   *   *

After years of walking in mid-Wales I thought I knew what birds to expect hereabouts. So it was with some astonishment one spring day that I looked down into a valley and saw, wheeling below me, a pair of birds that were new to me. But they were so much like outsize sparrowhawks I knew they had to be goshawks. The larger of the two, which I assumed was the female, circled with slow wing-beats just above the trees. But the male's behaviour was spectacular. He circled up and up, shrieking loudly, and then dived like an arrow at the female, turning up sharply just before reaching her. This exciting display he repeated seven or eight times. Then both hawks disappeared into the trees.

After that incident I went back there many times in the hope of seeing them again. Sometimes I was lucky, sometimes I was not. Then I got to know a falconer who was keen to release foreign goshawks in Wales and one day I went with him to liberate one. This was a 3½-year old female he had imported from Germany, a magnificent, very undomesticated bird he thought would do well in the wild. In thick cloud and rain we took her to the head of the valley where I had seen my original pair. Her jesses removed, she stood a

A buzzard with carrion crows feeding on a dead sheep in a snowy winter at Ynys Edwin.

moment on the falconer's gloved hand. Then she was gone into the mist.

After the elusiveness of goshawks let us be thankful for the obviousness of buzzards. There are well-known places on the Continent, such as Falsterbo in south Sweden, where in autumn you can see migrant buzzards flying south hour after hour, day after day. Our buzzards here are quite different, showing no desire to rise up on thermals and sail away to foreign lands. Instead each pair keeps to its own private patch all winter and doesn't usually have a lot to say to the buzzards next door. Yet even the most stand-offish seem to enjoy the odd brief sociable moment. In spring especially, a pair will be circling above their territory and for no obvious reason some of the neighbours will also rise and wheel round until soon there may be a dozen or so in the air. On rare occasions many more can be involved. My own highest count is thirty but others have reported seeing about forty weaving complex patterns all over the sky. These aerial gatherings, often accompanied by splendid buzzard music, do not usually last many minutes. Then the birds, as if satisfied that they have checked on each other, all drift quietly back home.

Another buzzard memory: almost anywhere in rural Wales a voice of late summer is the unmistakable wailing of young buzzards after they have left the nest. Normally we hear this hunger-cry through August and September and then no more. But one year there was an extraordinary exception to the rule: one of our local young buzzards wailed and followed its parents all through autumn and early winter until we were stricken by very severe weather in mid-December. By the time the thaw arrived we had quite forgotten our young buzzard but on the mild and misty morning of January 6, we heard the same old piteous cry from the pines close to our garden. Next day the parent buzzards were sailing about in courtship display, rejoicing in the warm sunshine; and the young one also flew round calling nearby. My records mention that on January 18 the cry of the young buzzard was 'still quite as distinctive as ever'. But that is the last mention of it.

★   ★   ★

Almost every year since Penny and I came to live in Wales our days, all through spring, have been lived on the closest terms with two little woodland birds we were hardly aware of in the Midlands of our youth. They are the redstart and the pied flycatcher; and though neither is blue they come close to being our bluebirds of happiness. They are totally unalike in their looks, in their voices and in the way they react to people. The stark black and white of the male pied flycatcher has nothing in common with the pink breast, grey-blue back and orange-red tail of the cock redstart. While the flycatcher often sings his simple up and down notes on quite low branches, the redstart's quavering trill is more likely to come from high in the tree tops, often a mere whispered sound caught in snatches on the breeze.

While the pied flycatcher is not afraid of being seen, the redstart prefers to be nothing more than a briefly glimpsed red tail crossing the wood path.

In our oak-shaded garden both of them use our nest-boxes, preferring those we fix on our bedroom window-sills where they are safe from stoats which are such a threat to boxes on trees. They often fight for these desirable homes. But one spring we had both of them nesting amicably a few yards apart at our windows. Then the boldness of the flycatchers and the elusiveness of the redstarts were never more striking. The male flycatcher stood on his box and sang even when we had tea on the terrace just below; but the male redstart became bold only when young had to be fed and even then it was a nervous sort of bravado. Every time he brought food he first perched on a nearby tree for several minutes before taking the plunge into his box. The furtiveness of female redstarts is astonishing. I am sure that people often have redstarts nesting in holes in their walls without ever noticing the birds at all. That could hardly happen with pied flycatchers.

*　　　*　　　*

Male pied flycatcher with, unusually, the brown plumage of a female.

173

As I leaf back through my diaries of the 1960s my eye is caught by a miscellany of unrelated incidents. There is a hare running away across Ynys Edwin marsh. After a hundred yards he stops, looks back and holds up a fore-paw which he shakes vigorously for a couple of seconds, exactly as if waving goodbye. Why does he do that? On the beach at Ynys-las we pick up a sea-horse about two inches long, dead and dry but perfect. Sea-horses belong to warmer waters and are rare along this coast. From our window on a sunny January day we have our best-ever view of a male sparrowhawk: we look up at him as he stands for five minutes on an oak bough that is covered in snow which emphasises the pinkness of his breast, throat and the sides of his neck; and, as always with sparrowhawks, the staring yellow eye. There is the August day when I watch a dozen or so purple hairstreaks at their courtship. I am on the ridge above Ynys Edwin where my eyes are level with the oak tops. The little butterflies, blackish above but sometimes scintillating with purple, are chasing each other wildly about, their flight close among the leaves or only just above them. Then they calm down and settle to sun themselves on the leaves, mostly head downwards, and the ballet is over.

My next vignette begins back in the cloudless summer of 1959 when Penny and I had just arrived at Ynys Edwin. Something we had in common with people all over the country that year was that in our garden we unexpectedly made the acquaintance of that strange plant, the thorn apple (*Datura stramonium*). Smelling decidedly evil, it stood over two feet tall, had large, toothed, oval leaves, mauve, trumpet-shaped flowers and big, spiny, green fruits. It was a product of the heat wave. Evidently its seeds lie dormant in the soil, cool summer after cool summer, waiting for a hot spell to start them into germination. Though we knew it to be poisonous it was a plant of such personality that we allowed it to live and drop its seeds to lie in wait for the next flaming summer. When that summer arrived years later, sure enough there was our thorn apple.

Another plant I made special note of in the 1960s was bog rosemary (*Andromeda polifolia*). It is rather rare in much of England and Wales but here in the west it is locally frequent and is especially common on Borth Bog. Its flowers are tiny, pale-pink bells which hang a few inches above the surface of the peat. As they normally appear in spring we were amazed when we crossed the bog looking for geese on November 21, 1967, to find the andromeda in full bloom. Two years later it again flowered well in November. Yet not one of our botany books mentions this twice-yearly flowering habit, if habit it is.

In November, 1968, there was a curious polecat incident. The story of the polecat in Wales in modern times has been phenomenal. Beginning the twentieth century as a rarity it is now widespread and abundant, even invading towns in the footsteps of the fox. It lives in most types of country and eats mammals, birds, frogs, anything it can catch. Carrion too, and this would explain why a friend of ours, walking by the sea at Tywyn, found a polecat (very much alive) which had caught itself in a lobster-pot washed up on the beach!

Let me end this chapter with two rare birds of the 1960s. In June, 1967, I am motoring through Caernarfonshire with Cecil Lambourne. We are passing a little marsh just west of Pen-y-groes when a bird on a roadside wire seems interesting. We stop to look and through binoculars see that it matches perfectly the field-guide description of the lesser grey shrike. It is the first county record of this rarity. Two years later, on the Dyfi estuary, comes a new species for Cardiganshire: in mid-November, 1969, a small wader defeats my efforts to identify it until it walks out of the water and shows its shanks to be brightest yellow. Others see it later and eventually it is named as a lesser yellow-legs which has somehow found its way across the broad Atlantic.

Chapter 11

1970 brought momentous changes to us here on the Dyfi estuary. Most of the tidal part of the river had just been declared a National Nature Reserve and now the adjacent Ynys-hir estate had been bought by the Royal Society for the Protection of Birds. As one who had long helped the late owner, Hubert Mappin, to maintain the property as a private bird sanctuary, I took on the job of wardening the new reserve, preparing trails through the woods and across the fields, building hides so that birds could be seen but not disturbed, and re-creating the pools and marshes of former days. It would have taken years to carry out these projects on my own but as soon as the word got around that help was needed, volunteers of all ages, youngsters especially, came flocking in, often travelling great distances, to put in enormously long hours and expend vast energy to get everything done. It was a most heartening manifestation of goodwill towards a deserving cause.

The reserve's first official visitors I remember well—ten keen members of the London Natural History Society who came on Easter Monday, March 30. They had a good day which began with two sparrowhawks circling in a pair-bond display just overhead. Our London visitors also heard the year's first chiff-chaffs and greenshanks, had close views of a hen harrier and listened to an exceptionally early tree pipit. Finally they saw what they had most wanted to see—a flock of Greenland white-fronted geese filling the air with wild music as they flew past up the estuary.

One of the first hides built at Ynys-hir, skilfully erected for us by the Venture Scouts and since much enlarged, looks intimately across the estuary at one of its narrowest points. It has always been a favourite among the reserve's regular visitors, some of whom sit there for hours entranced not only by the birds but also by the tides as they ebb and flow past the hide, and by the wide views across the saltings away to the far-off hills. Herons, cormorants, ducks, waders, dabchicks: some of these are usually visible; and there is ever the chance of other birds passing up or down the river—birds of prey, kingfishers, gulls, terns and occasional rarer ones wandering in from the sea. Sometimes there is the sudden splash of sea trout or salmon; and watchers have, very rarely, reported otters and even porpoises and seals.

One day a group of us saw a merlin chasing a kingfisher up and down that stretch of the river. Many times the merlin overtook the kingfisher and was about to snatch it in mid-air when the kingfisher, with perfect timing, dived into the water, popped up a second or two later and doubled back the way it had come, only to find the merlin had also turned back and was still in hot pursuit. This high-speed chase went on for long minutes but in the end we were relieved to see the merlin give up and disappear down river. I think we all felt that kingfishers are too precious to become a lunch item for predators.

In that first spring the reserve welcomed a stream of visitors who came mainly to see woodland birds which are commoner in Wales than in the Midlands and southern England, notably pied flycatcher,

Hen harrier, recovered from illness, being released by Penny at Ynys-hir Reserve in October 1971.

A heron from Norway which was fed for a while on sardines at the RSPB
reserve, Ynys-hir, before it continued on its migration.

wood warbler and redstart. But a party in May soon lost interest in the birds. They were thirty-two members of the Federation of Ontario Naturalists on a tour of British reserves. When I led them into one of our oakwoods there were whoops of delight which puzzled me until I realised that none of them had ever seen bluebells in the mass before. They were totally enraptured by the fragrant blue sheet of flowers that spread before them away into the depths of the wood. As one of them explained, they had all heard about British bluebell woods but never imagined such a stirring sight as this. For the next ten minutes there was a continuous clicking of cameras as bluebells were photographed from every possible angle. I remember wondering how many of the pictures would be a disappointment. Bluebells are not always easy to photograph. Even with the films of today they may come out pink or mauve rather than blue and the problem was even worse in those days.

Among the delights of looking after a nature reserve were those visitors who brought in specimens or who found animals on the reserve we had no idea were here. There was policeman Ken Williams of Anglesey who brought us a hen harrier which he had nursed back to health and which he wished to be released on a bird reserve. There was the young man who arrived with an exhausted heron in a box on the back of his motor-bike. It was a particularly interesting heron because on its leg was a ring that had been put on it in a nest in Norway earlier that year. (Till then we had assumed that all the herons we saw here were 'our' herons.) This bird soon became quite tame on a diet of sardines in oil and would wait on the roof-top until the next tin was opened. Gradually he learnt to find his own food on the estuary but he came back every few days for a sardine hand-out before he finally went on his way.

Another cardboard-box exhibit was brought here by a visitor who came to show me four spectacular caterpillars which he had found eating lady's bedstraw in the dunes at Aberdyfi. These fully grown larvae of the rare migrant bedstraw hawkmoth brought back for me all the thrill I used to feel in my childhood when I found my first caterpillars of poplar and lime hawkmoths along the leafy suburban roads of Harborne and Edgbaston.

Then there was the harvest mouse episode for which we were indebted to our friend Libby Lenton of the Vincent Wildlife Trust. Libby specialised in otters but bubbled over with enthusiasm for other mammals as well. She became a frequent visitor to Ynys-hir, tracing signs of otters and surveying our population of shrews, voles and fieldmice. Her greatest triumph was when she took me to one of our marshes and said: 'Let's look for harvest mice'. In the very first tussock of purple moorgrass she looked into was a harvest mouse nest! Until that moment no one had ever suspected that we might have this smallest of all British rodents at Ynys-hir.

1970 was our summer of the little egret, a bird that was then far scarcer in Britain than it is today. This elegant white creature was first spotted on the estuary on June 22, walking along the water's edge at low tide, snapping at small fish in the shallows—a momentous event because never before had an egret been known here. Next day it had gone and for a week we looked for it in vain. Then it was back, passing at dusk in leisurely flight above the saltings at the head of the estuary, over on the Meirionnydd side. Soon it circled round, crossed the river and flew into the pines where Ynys-hir's herons always have their nests.

An egret, after all, is of the heron cousinhood, so this one evidently assumed that a heronry was its proper roosting place. Maybe it had wandered here from some southern land where various species of herons and egrets are quite used to breeding and roosting together. But the grey herons of Ynys-hir, unused to such cosmopolitanism, immediately drove this pure-white outsider straight back across the river where it vanished into the darkness. Many such vagrants are here today, gone tomorrow. Not so our 1970 egret. It must have found an acceptable roost somewhere and had also decided that the estuary was a good enough feeding ground, for it stayed here about two months, a welcome reminder of life in warmer latitudes.

That summer of the egret was also a merganser summer. It is a curious habit of mergansers and shelducks that as soon as they get their baby ducklings to the water they may merge them with other broods and leave them in the care of just one or two females. We found this happening at Ynys-hir as soon as mergansers began breeding here in some numbers. First we saw two broods unite to

A brood of mergansers led by their mother. Bird second from left is a black-necked grebe. Ynys-hir RSPB reserve, August 1970.

form a flock of about two dozen. Then the two dozen acquired more and more recruits until the day came when an adult female swam past with more than forty young ones in line astern. A few days later we were astonished to find that mother merganser was now in charge of seventy lively offspring. Was this a record, we wondered. We ought to have read our books more carefully. Then we would have known that in Ireland (if you can believe Irish stories) someone once saw hundreds of young mergansers in one crèche with only two nursemaids on duty. What I would love to know is how these adult females get landed with these responsibilities and do they work on a rota system?

A matter of routine on a bird reserve is to make regular counts of the birds. Some species are difficult, not wanting you to know that they are there at all. Others are self-advertising and easy. And there are those that vary with the seasons. For instance, we often found great spotted woodpeckers could be very elusive all winter but in spring some individuals became quite bold and would hack out their nesting holes in full view of spectators and later feed their young with equal publicity. Even the more cautious pairs eventually had their nest holes betrayed by the continuous cacophony of the young ones yelling to be fed.

181

Several of these woodpecker holes involved us in an intriguing little mystery. In June, a few days after the young woodpeckers had flown, we heard squeaks coming persistently from the vacated holes. To explain them we could only think of bats. So we placed a ladder against one of the trees and found a volunteer to stand on top of it as the light began to fade after sunset. There he waited quietly, holding a butterfly net over the hole and in no time at all he had caught a noctule bat as it came out. Exactly the same happened at several other woodpecker nests, not only that June but in subsequent years as well. It was strange to think of those noctules waiting patiently every June for the young woodpeckers to get airborne.

It is a fascination on summer evenings to look up at the apex of our roof and see the bats emerge, not big noctules but little pipistrelles. One after another out they come and flutter off into the dark and usually we have no idea where they go or what they find to eat. Very occasionally, however, we have actually seen them in action. Catching ghost moths, for instance. Ghost moths are worth seeing when, in the June dusk, the males go through their courtship display—white, spectral little creatures swinging from side to side as they dance a few feet above the ground. This pirouetting, though so beautiful and so attractive to the female moths, is fraught with danger. We have seen our pipistrelles snapping up dancing ghost moths quite close to our faces as we peered through the gloaming. Later in the summer our long-eared bats prey on those pretty moths called yellow underwings. We have never seen them do it but we find the moths' discarded wings in our outbuildings underneath bat roosts.

'I saw a fine specimen of *Vanessa antiope* near Llyn Ogwen but did not secure it.' In these words Samuel Price of Birmingham reported in *The Zoologist* seeing a Camberwell beauty in the heart of Snowdonia on June 30, 1854. Seldom does this spectacular Continental butterfly get as far as Wales but I remember in the 1970s a couple of people arriving at Ynys-hir full of a thrilling story. They had been picknicking on the storm beach at Borth when they noticed a large, dark butterfly coming in off the sea. Magically it settled on a stone just beside them. 'Look', said the wife, who was no entomologist, 'there's your butterfly!' Her husband had to agree; it was unmistakably 'his' butterfly. He worked for a firm that made 'Butterfly Brand' stationery goods (I have a packet of their gummed labels on my table as I write) and their products are adorned with their logo, the dark-purple, pale-edged Camberwell beauty. Though the husband admitted to me that he had no more knowledge of butterflies than his wife had, their story had a real ring of truth. Later I heard that other Camberwell beauties were reported in Wales that summer. What wouldn't I have given to have seen one!

An early visitor to the RSPB reserve at Ynys-hir was unusual. He was a small boy who made it clear from the start that his interest in birds came second to his devotion to butterflies. That day he wished above all to be shown one he had read about but never seen—the purple hairstreak. Even on a sunny day this is not always an easy butterfly to find because, although quite common in our oakwoods here, it has the frustrating habit of keeping to the tree-tops and is normally only visible when it occasionally flutters above the highest leaves.

The weather that day was unfortunate. It had been very dull all morning and just as we were setting off in pursuit of purple hairstreaks it began to rain. The boy's parents were for turning back but the boy himself was so piteously disappointed that I decided we must go on and try a little trick I had once seen work with perfect success on just such a day. We walked to the top of an oak-covered slope from where we looked down onto the trees. I then picked up a few sticks and threw them one after another into the tops of the nearest oak. Nothing happened at first but, with the seventh or eighth stick, out flew two or three very small blackish butterflies which immediately vanished back among the leaves. So, very briefly and distantly, my young friend had seen his first purple hairstreaks. I hope after all these years he still remembers that wet day at Ynys-hir.

★   ★   ★

In the spring of 1970, some of Aberdyfi's herring gulls made an unprecedented move: they spread a few miles up the estuary and began breeding on little man-made cliffs along the railway between Aberdyfi and Dyfi Junction. They even overflowed onto the line itself, where I saw one nest actually built against the outside of one of the rails. I waited to see what would happen when a train came along: the gull sitting on the nest merely fluttered off a few feet then returned to her eggs as soon as the train had passed. All that summer the railway workers took pride in their new gull colony and gave it every protection. It was their contribution to European Conservation Year.

★   ★   ★

June 19, 1970, was a good botanical day. A group of us, including indefatigable Mary Richards, then aged 85, were scrambling up Cwm Cywarch, a steep valley in the Aran range east of Dolgellau. It was a hot day, too hot for most of us but just right for Mary after her years in south-central Africa. The valley is one of those special places, quite rare in upland Wales, where the rocks are lime-rich and the mountain flora varied. So we had no difficulty in finding good plants like brittle bladder fern and green spleenwort; mountain sorrel and lesser meadow-rue; roseroot, globe flower and mossy saxifrage. Then we struggled up a troublesome scree to the foot of spectacular cliffs and were pleased to see a few early purple orchids still in flower though they were long over in the lowlands. A good end to our day's herborising, we thought, for in the mountains this is quite a rare plant.

Yet the day was not quite over. There was an excited yell of 'albida' from Mary Richards and soon we clustered round the great find of the day—a single spike of that rarity, the small white orchid (*Pseudorchis albida*) which, alas, gets ever harder to find as the years go by.

★   ★   ★

A raven entertained me greatly one day as he flew by while I was botanising in Cwm Glas Mawr on Snowdon. Ravens are very good at aerobatics, their favourite trick being to turn over and fly upside down for a brief moment before righting themselves. This Snowdon raven not only turned tummy upwards six times in quick succession but also gave a loud croak each time he was upside down. When I see

184

ravens at these clownish performances I can't help feeling that they are simply having fun; but I suppose that sooner or later some solemn biologist will explain it all in scientific terms.

What about the ravens' many other noises? They remind me of the raven roost that used to be at Machynlleth. It was in a grove of old Scots pines on a hill-top just outside the town and it could be approached by a zigzag path hidden in a spruce plantation. In the cover of these conifers I could often get near enough to the ravens (there were many scores of them summer and winter) to hear their repertoire of chuckles, squeaks, croonings and deep mumblings which they uttered in chorus just before going to sleep along the pine boughs.

Visiting that raven roost year after year (it persisted for decades) I came to realise that it was really much more than a roost. Those hill-top pines were in fact a permanent hub of raven society. The population was greatest at night but you could go up there any hour of the day, any day of the year, and there would always be some ravens present. Probably they gathered here because Machynlleth had its rubbish dump nearby where they could pick up scraps just as ravens did in the streets of medieval London where they squabbled for food with kites, cats, dogs and countless pigs. Machynlleth no longer has a rubbish dump. It no longer has a raven commune either and so, alas, no more mass acrobatics, no more *eisteddfodau* just at dusk.

★   ★   ★

One year in late March I saw two kites perform an astonishing manoeuvre. I was on a round of possible nesting sites and was walking up a valley to a hillside oakwood where kites had often bred. As I passed the wood it seemed deserted yet when I turned to look back I saw, to my surprise, not one but two pairs of kites circling over the trees and diving about in great excitement, even using their lovely whistling call which is not heard all that often. Then two of them (I presume they were both males or both females) met high in the air, grasped each other's talons and twirled round in a wild dance, at the same time falling like a stone until they almost reached the tree-tops where they quickly disengaged. A few minutes later they went through exactly the same performance, the whole episode, as before, taking only three seconds. I had read of such talon-locking performances by other large birds-of-prey but they have seldom been reported among the kites of Wales.

This incident took my mind back to a tragedy of a few years before. I received a report of a kite found with a broken wing in a beechwood where I knew there was a nest. Gloomily I went to investigate. There was nothing I disliked more than having to decide what to do about birds with broken wings. There were no bird hospitals available in those days and the best we could hope for was to find a sympathetic vet. The kite was lying on a carpet of brown beech leaves right under her newly built nest. She had obviously struggled for hours to get airborne and had twisted that wing so many times it was now a shapeless bunch of dirty feathers. I was puzzled at the time how that kite could have broken her wing. But after seeing the reckless way rival kites can drop out of the sky, spinning round with their talons grasped together, I could understand how easily they might fracture a wing against a branch.

If kites can act so strangely in March, who dares to predict what hares will get up to? They are well known for standing up on their hind legs and boxing with each other; and more than once I have had a hare come running straight towards me and pass within a few feet without even seeing me. Then one spring a hare developed another eccentricity. Some mother hares will not take the risk of putting all their harelets into one basket. Instead they hide one in a rush patch, another behind a bramble, a third under a hedge and so on. In the first week of March, 1975, I was astonished early one morning when I first went out into the garden, to see a hare go leaping away from under a shrub a few yards from our back door. Never before had I seen a hare so near the house and I wondered what was going on. When I looked under that shrub I found a newly born leveret, furry, open-eyed and precocious yet so young.

Though we didn't want hares in the garden any more than we wanted rabbits, Penny and I couldn't help feeling honoured that the normally so timid hare had beaten a pathway nearly to our door and then given birth. Rightly she judged her babe would be safer here from buzzards and other predators; and no doubt she had made sure that we kept neither cat nor dog. Four days she tended her offspring under that shrub. Several times we saw her slip in extremely furtively and depart with equal caution. Then on the fifth morning the infant, now much grown and very alert, was led out of the garden and away into the marshy fields. For the leveret it was a beginning. For us it was an ending and we felt quite bereft.

That year brought the sadness of seeing our old friend Hugh Chater buried in the steep, far-seeing graveyard overlooking Llanbadarn Fawr, Aberystwyth. July 1, 1975, was a hot, sunny, still day, the only sound of nature, as we came out of the church, being the song of a collared dove. Appropriately it reminded me of the voice of another kind of collared dove, the mourning dove of Africa, whose melancholy notes are inseparable from my memories of breathlessly hot October days at the bottom of the Great Rift Valley. As we stood at Hugh's graveside a chiff-chaff in a nearby tree sang a requiem *fortissimo*. So we said goodbye to our first botanical mentor to whom we had long been in the habit of reporting whatever interesting plants or other treasures we happened to find.

★   ★   ★

If you move west from Shrewsbury by road or rail you soon see, miles ahead, a group of monadnock hills rising abruptly beyond the Shropshire plain. These triple heights of Breidden are like a delegation meeting you at the frontier to announce the mountains of Wales. It was in July, 1975, that I first got acquainted with Breidden, under the guidance of the eminent Shropshire naturalist, Charles Sinker. Charles told me about the special ecology of Breidden, its unique lime-rich dolerite rocks and the rare plants known there since the days of Edward Lhuyd in the 1680s: spiked speedwell (*Veronica spicata*), sticky catchfly (*Lychnis viscaria*) and rock cinquefoil (*Potentilla rupestris*). On that same day Charles took me up another notable Welsh border hill—Corndon. There, in contrast with Breidden, the soils were acid and fit mainly for heather and bilberry and, here at almost its most easterly station in southern Britain, a luxuriance of parsley fern.

Two years later I was again on Breidden, this time at a meeting of the Montgomeryshire Field Society. It was a cold April day but siskins and goldfinches seemed to be enjoying it as they sang in a mixed choir in the ash trees up the slopes. On the summit, botanist Doris Pugh pointed to the numerous spring ephemerals growing in the very thin soils; and geologist Mary Hignett didn't seem to notice how chilly the wind was as she enthusiastically described the rocks about us. The Montgomeryshire Field Society has always prided itself on its well-attended field frolics and this day was typical: lots of people got to the top, including one elderly blind man assisted by a guide dog which itself looked rather weighed down with years.

*   *   *

A rare bird I have never yet seen in Wales or anywhere else is that beautiful little plover, the dotterel. I have looked out for dotterels, spring and autumn, on many a Welsh mountain because when on passage they have the unique habit of moving from one peak to another and feeding awhile before flying on again. Nowhere has luck been on my side. I have, for instance, spent whole days in September, plodding the length and breadth of the Plynlimon moorlands in a profitless pursuit of dotterels. Yet other people can go up there and see a dozen or more.

In mid-August, 1975, I stayed a night or two near Brecon under the roof of a friend of many years, Eric Bartlett, who had a vast knowledge of Breconshire's birds and who was keen to show me round his beloved county. He happened to mention that two dotterel had been seen in August of the preceding year on the top of Hay Bluff. So when he asked me next morning where I would like to be taken I had no doubt at all. It was a wondrous day, windstill, warm and sunny; and the whole top of Hay Bluff was fragrant with heather. Bees had come up in their thousands, honey bees and bumbles, and their music was everywhere. There was something else, something I had never seen before. Down in the lowlands there must have been a prodigious hatching of small tortoiseshell butterflies which, presumably summoned by the scent of the heather, had, like the bees, come up from far away to sip at the nectar. Wherever we looked these paint-fresh beauties fluttered over the moorland in scores. In a world where so many butterflies are on the retreat this was a heartening manifestation of life still abounding. Eric and I long remembered that perfect day on Hay Bluff. We had felt no need of dotterels.

Eric took me to another of his favourite haunts—the beautiful Llyn Syfaddan at Llangorse, the biggest natural lake in south Wales. I had been there thirteen years before, my companions then being those endearing, almost inseparable botanists, Irene Vaughan of Carmarthenshire and Tommie Warren Davis of Pembrokeshire. Then we had found the lake's shallows patched with the elegant small leaves and yellow flowers of the fringed water-lily. There were sedges I had never seen before. The great reedmace and the small reedmace grew near each other, each in its separate depth of water. We had seen floating mats of water bistort and submerged thickets of water milfoil. Reed warblers sang everywhere. Yellow wagtails fluttered into the air catching flies for their young. Coots, grebes and other fowl were many. It was an idyllic scene with every prospect, it seemed, of going on from everlasting to everlasting.

But now after the lapse of years, there was every sign of deterioration. For though the water-lilies were still there, and the reedmaces, the sedges, the reed warblers and the wagtails, there were now boats everywhere, including power-boats and water-skiers. And the water, Eric told me, had become so polluted with nitrates draining in off the neighbouring farmlands, that botanists were no longer able to discover several rare plants which formerly flourished in the lake. Ever since that day, struggles have gone on to try to save this lake which ought to have been declared a National Nature Reserve long ago but never has been.

★   ★   ★

1976 was an unforgettable year that began with a rare tidal surge. December, 1975, had ended in a turmoil of wind and rain and the new year was only two days old when the evening tide came up the estuary with more than a full gale behind it. With deluges of rain on the mountains, the Dyfi had risen quickly and when the swollen river met the swollen tide we had the biggest flood anyone could remember.

In several places the railway bank alongside the estuary was swept entirely away for hundreds of yards, leaving the rails hanging in the air and grotesquely buckled. Three RSPB hides along the estuary were never seen again. After the storm the fields and woods were deeply under water for nearly a week and we thought of all the small mammals that we assumed had been drowned. Yet after the flood had drained away we found not a single corpse. And when we set live-traps to catch fieldmice, voles and shrews we caught just as many as before the flood. This I could not understand and it puzzles me still.

That record flood of January, 1976, was followed months later by such a drought that at the end of August the rain gauge showed an incredible zero for a month that usually has plenty of wet days. There is a poignancy about some of our memories of those harsh months when the sun shone so pitilessly. We looked with foreboding at some splendid old beeches on a steep hillside near us: as early as mid-August their leaves were already shrivelling. We knew that slope: it was nothing but a tilted plate of rock covered by a thin soil from which all trace of moisture must long ago have vanished. The drought ended at last but the autumn rain came too late to save those beeches. Next April many stood leafless and dead.

I have another memory from that burning summer—of walking through acres of bracken already dried up and brown in the middle of August; then through a wood of hazels, birches, rowans and hawthorns, all with their leaves withered and falling. Outside the wood was a ditch that normally has two or three feet of water in it. Now it was absolutely dry and on the desiccated mud of its bed lay ten eels about two feet long, stiff and apparently quite dead. But I had heard of the tenacity of life possessed by eels. So I took these ten and put them into a nearby pool. Before my eyes there was a miraculous resurrection: in a few minutes the eels began to show signs of life and one by one they went wriggling away down in the dark forests of water milfoil that lay in the depths.

An athletic frog and a high-speed snake were also part of the drought of 1976. I was in a narrow gully between rock walls when a big yellow frog came leaping past me in an unmistakeable state of frenzy. That he took no notice of me was not surprising because he was followed in about three seconds by the fastest grass snake I have ever seen. Unlike the frog, the snake did see me because I made an instinctive move to stand in his way to protect the frog. The snake stopped and made much play with his tongue while he sized up the situation; then he turned and went slowly back the way he had come. I don't suppose snakes chase frogs with such urgency very often; but during a heat-wave frogs presumably retire into aestivation and become very hard to find even by the hungriest serpents.

The same heat-wave brought an astonishing irruption of 7-spot ladybirds. It happened on July 7 and was very sudden. One minute all was normal as I walked across a field at Ynys-hir. The next minute the air was full of these little flying red beetles that were dropping to the turf all about me. It was a deluge, a cloud-burst of ladybirds. People arriving from the coast four miles away told the same story: Ynys-las beach and dunes were covered with ladybirds apparently coming in over the sea. A group of young volunteers doing conservation tasks in the sand dunes had to stop work for a while because they were so beetle-smothered. Children playing on the sands were screaming with terror. People got into their cars and roared away in panic. Yet in less than sixty minutes the whole insect multitude had taken off, never to be heard of again.

That year another insect acted strangely: for a very brief spell, purple hairstreaks became almost as familiar as peacocks or tortoise-shells. These hairstreaks are believed to feed mainly on 'honey-dew' which is a euphemism for the sweet and sticky excreta which aphids in their millions deposit all over the oak leaves. So satisfied are the purple hairstreaks by this ambrosial diet that normally they do not descend to human levels to visit either wildflowers or garden flowers. But for several days in mid-August, 1976—the only time I have ever seen this happen—the purple hairstreaks were often in our garden seeking nectar from buddleias and other scented shrubs. I assume that for once the honey-dew harvest had failed because the aphids had all dried up and perished in that never-to-be-forgotten summer.

★ ★ ★

In June, 1976, I got this note from Gwen Moffat, the well-known climber, writer and Snowdonian mountain guide whom we had known since our youth-hostel wardening days in 1946: 'At 5 p.m. on

Monday the 14th', wrote Gwen, 'a grey squirrel was eating crumbs on the summit of Crib Goch. Is 3,023 feet a record? One glimpse, then he went over the edge on the Cwm Glas side. I watched him for about half a minute scampering across very steep rocks. Where does he live or spend the night? Are squirrels starting to build dreys in holes in rocks?' This was only one letter amongst several I received from various people about that time, telling of grey squirrels seen in the uplands, all the way from Snowdonia to the Brecon Beacons. As far as I know, this mountaineering was something new in British grey squirrel history and was evidently a result of a population explosion. These adventurous individuals carrying, as it were, the banner 'Excelsior', were pioneers aspiring to advance the frontiers of grey squirreldom by winning new lands beyond the mountains. This they did with huge success and soon they were masters of pretty well the whole of Wales.

*   *   *

In these conservation-minded days we hear much talk of helping struggling species by introducing them to fresh habitats when their rightful homes have been destroyed. It is a meritorious idea but not always easy to put into practice, as we discovered at Ynys-hir in 1977-9. The experiment began by accident on March 30, 1977. I was passing near Borth Bog when I saw smoke and flames spreading across an area that I knew was a haunt of the marsh fritillary, a little butterfly which, though still well established locally in parts of Wales, is getting scarce in Britain as a whole. I knew that the tiny caterpillars, just emerged from their winter rest, should be feeding at that season and I soon found a whole web of them on a plant of devil's-bit scabious. With the advancing fire only a few yards away I decided those caterpillars had better be transferred to our marsh at Ynys-hir where there was plenty of the scabious but no marsh fritillaries. To protect them from ichneumon flies, I reared these larvae at home in jam jars where they eventually changed into prettily marked pupae and were released as butterflies in our marsh. There were about thirty in all.

In the days that followed it was a joy to go down to the marsh on a sunny morning and see these deep-orange fritillaries on the wing;

The marsh fritillary was introduced at Ynys-hir RSPB reserve in a rescue operation in 1977, but the experiment failed.

and if we approached carefully we could see the females laying eggs on the underside of the scabious leaves. I was full of hope for this experiment until the day I told Peter Crow about it. Peter was a butterfly expert from north Wales and much experienced with marsh fritillaries. His comment was chilling: 'Yes, they'll do all right for a year or two till the ichneumons find them. Then they'll fizzle out. The conditions can't be quite right for them on your marsh or they'd be there already'. But when I went back to the marsh and saw the fritillaries flying about so happily I felt there was a good chance that this time an expert would be proved wrong.

The following June was an exciting time. There were many fritillaries over the marsh and some were obviously laying. On June 17 we tried to count the eggs but gave up when we reached a thousand. The future looked really good and I day-dreamed of the fabulous number of butterflies we would see there in another year's time. In the event nothing of the sort happened. June, 1979, produced hardly any and not one has ever been seen since. The doomspeak of Peter Crow had been correct.

Chapter 12

When that unique man, George Borrow, climbed Plynlimon in 1854, he made three rivers his own by visiting their sources. First he made his way to the cliff-shadowed lake that is the source of the Rheidol. From there he walked to the morassy springs of the Severn which he thought 'rather a shabby source for so notable a stream'. Then two miles south he came to where the Wye leaps more cleanly from the hillside. To use his quaint expression, he 'took possession' of these rivers by drinking at their birth springs. With that ritual he was perhaps expressing what we all feel to some degree when at last we get to a place we have long wanted to visit: subconsciously we 'take possession' of it. Certainly I felt that way in 1978 when I landed for the first time on Puffin Island under the guidance of Dr Richard Arnold, the leading expert on the island's ecology.

Puffin Island, Anglesey, home of many seabirds.

Puffin is a high hump of grey limestone, three-quarters of a mile long, close to the eastern tip of Anglesey. It is defended all round by cliffs or steep slopes, is privately owned and has been uninhabited by people for many years. So what met our group when we landed there on June 3 was a yodelling mob of herring gulls. All that day we were never out of the din of those gulls and they shouted what sounded very much like a triumphant goodbye to us as we left. In the preceding years there had been a huge upsurge in herring gull numbers everywhere and here on Puffin was the biggest colony in Wales, their crowded nests spread over a large area of bare slope on the west side of the island.

Puffin had surprises. The tall vegetation for instance. I was used to the treeless nudity of Skokholm, Skomer, Bardsey and St Tudwal's; but here on Puffin there was an astonishing twenty-acre forest of elder covering a third of the island. As well as elder there were jungles of nettles, alexanders and cow parsley, some of them freakishly tall, presumably because intensively fertilised by bird-droppings. Summer, we were told by our leader, would bring a huge growth of burdock. Another wonder was the total absence of rabbits. Most of our off-shore islands have long had rabbits in thousands, the descendants of those introduced in medieval times. Puffin, too, once had its rabbits but they were wiped out, every one of them, when myxomatosis came in the mid-1950s—a very rare example of a population entirely eliminated by that disease.

Puffin Island got its name in the days when it was spectacularly an island of puffins. Today it may as well go back to one of its earlier names, Priestholm or Ynys Seiriol, for the puffin multitudes have dwindled, no one knows why. Too many rats perhaps. Certainly there were many rat-holes as we climbed towards the north end of the island. But nearby we also saw small groups of puffins nesting in holes on the same slopes. We also soon realised that though the puffins had declined so desperately, the island was still a real seabird island as distinct from a mere gull island. Round the cliffs were many breeding guillemots, razorbills, fulmars, cormorants, shags and about a thousand pairs of kittiwakes. I was also pleased to find one of my favourite little ferns, the lanceolate spleenwort, looking very prosperous along the horizontal crevices of the cliffs. I was intrigued to see it growing in limestone. Till then I had supposed it to be a lime-avoider because it never seems to grow on lime-mortared walls along with rusty-back fern, wall rue and maidenhair spleenwort. But the natural world is full of such surprises.

That spring I was able to 'take possession' not only of Puffin Island but also of Flat Holm, an island in the murky waters of the Bristol Channel, six miles off the coast near Cardiff. Flat Holm I remember as another citadel of gulls. There was a multitude of nesting herring gulls on the cliffs, and a huge colony, mainly of lesser blackbacks, spread out over the level top of the island on ground that had at one time been arable land. Those hundreds of birds sitting calmly on their nests in an ocean of bluebells and white scurvy-grass would have made a peaceful idyll if the air had not been full of their screaming, yelling mates which repeatedly dive-bombed all human intruders, knocking the hats off some, drawing blood on the bald pates of others.

There was more to Flat Holm than gulls. In our Bristol University party who crossed that day from Weston-super-Mare there was a young man who specialised in reptiles and was soon producing slow worms and lizards like rabbits from a hat. Both, he demonstrated, were Flat Holm specialities: the slow worms a richer blue, the lizards a darker brown, than those on the mainland. Since that time the gull population has fluctuated on Flat Holm and elsewhere because of disease. In all species, including our own, over-population must inevitably bring its problems.

Next year yet another island: for a week in October, 1979, I was on Ynys Dewi (Ramsey Island) in Pembrokeshire with three friends, R. S. Thomas, Elfyn Pugh and Robin Pratt. At that time Robin, who was living on the island, had a herd of red deer, magnificent creatures that kept away from us, often standing on the distant skyline in splendid poses. But during out stay the stags came into rut, threatening each other (and us) with their roaring voices and challenging postures and by the end of the week it was us who were keeping away from them.

Compared with flat-topped Skokholm and Skomer, Ramsey, with its two high humps, is almost mountainous, a rewarding subject for artists and photographers perched on St David's Head. Geologists

Ynys Dewi (Ramsey Island), Pembrokeshire, an RSPB Reserve.

love Ramsey for its mixture of Ordovician rocks, some sedimentary and containing fossils, some igneous, both acid and basic. Ramsey is spectacularly savage at the south end where it breaks off into islets with fine cliffs up which white waves burst and foam in the south-west gales. Between the island and the mainland a line of fang-like rocks called the Bitches stretches nearly half-way across the sound and through them the greater tides roar like a river in flood.

We went to Ramsey for the birds and day after day we hoped for a great passage of migrants; but throughout the week there was the merest trickle of warblers, wagtails and flycatchers. Seven jays, unusual on passage, were strange to see hopping about the summit rocks of this treeless island. Bird of the week was unquestionably the osprey which stayed several days, diving into the duck-pond by the farmhouse and carrying away several sizeable fish. It was too late in the year for us to see the rarer plants for which Ramsey is known: fiddle dock, yellow centaury, balm-leaved figwort, small pondweed and others. But the royal fern was in good shape in gullies going down to the sea and so were the prostrate juniper bushes which, though I was familiar with them on the Snowdonian uplands, I had never before seen on sea cliffs. Two choice little ferns adorned the ledges: sea spleenwort which is thinly scattered round much of the Welsh coast; and the more local lanceolate spleenwort which I had not seen since I was on Puffin Island.

A lasting memory of Ramsey must be of seals and choughs, both of which love the caverns that penetrate far underneath the island. It was the seals' breeding season and on practically every beach we looked down at their fat, white, furry pups, lying on the shingle, sometimes alone, sometimes being suckled by their mothers. While Ramsey has long been the seal metropolis of Wales it is also the best Welsh island for choughs. Perhaps a dozen pairs had nested that year and now they and their young were the commonest birds. And what more endearing companions could we have wished for than these cheerful-voiced choughs busily pecking into the turf wherever we went or showing off their acrobatics over the cliffs?

After a week Elfyn and I came home but R. S. Thomas stayed another fortnight. Migration improved and in all he managed to log ninety-four species, among them great northern diver, sooty shearwater, ring-tailed harrier, merlin, both the godwits, arctic skua, Mediterranean gull, short-eared owl, firecrest, black redstart, corn bunting and twite. In 1992 came the good news that Ramsey had been bought by the RSPB. So its conservation is now as secure as it can be in an area of the coast so threatened by the possibility of oil-tanker wrecks and by pollution caused by off-shore oil drilling.

★   ★   ★

1979 was a year to remember for stripping the leaves off our oaks. At the beginning of June the trees were green. By the end of it they were black. Caterpillars on oaks are common enough but even in a bad year some trees escape pretty well unscathed. Not so in 1979. The whole of our nearest wood was defoliated from end to end by larvae of the winter moth which then went on to achieve something I had never seen before—they laid bare even sycamores and sweet chestnuts. But what put the finishing touch to an already amazing performance was to see those millions of little devourers descending on silken threads to gnaw away at the leathery leaves of rhododendrons which are hardly ever nibbled by anything. After less severe June plagues the oaks usually find the strength to grow more leaves in late summer. That year the wood remained bare and winter-like from the end of June till the following spring.

The same spring brought an incident I hesitate to mention because I know no one will believe it. Yet it really happened one April morning when I was leaning out of a bedroom window fixing a nest-box on the wall. I was hammering in the last nail when a blue tit, instantly followed by another, literally brushed past my arm and disappeared into the box! Such enterprise certainly deserved to succeed. But when nesting holes are in short supply there is no saying what will happen. In the event those blue tits were soon evicted by pied flycatchers who in turn were quickly dispossessed by redstarts. Spring days are full of such dramas.

That was also the year when we had a flightless raven here. Its wing presumably broken in a flying accident, it survived for several months living a secretive life in the fields and woods round Ynys Edwin, seldom venturing from the shelter of trees or gorse bushes. If ever I happened to meet with it in the open it hopped clumsily but quite quickly back into cover. It always looked well fed and I was beginning to think it would be our neighbour for years; but one day I was saddened to find it dead. I brought home one of its largest feathers, a trophy I treasure to this day. I know ravens are supposed to be black but this feather has a bright-blue sheen worthy of some bird of the tropics.

There was a moment later in autumn which reminded me of this grounded raven and provided a possible explanation of how it may have broken its wing. Ravens tend to go a little hysterical in October. They are very early nesters and already in autumn they are getting excited about the breeding season. They chase each other wildly about overhead, turning on their backs even more than usual and often using very strong language. One morning, as I motored along a lane, two ravens came hurtling out of the sky ahead and very nearly crashed into my windscreen, sweeping up and over it at the last split second. It seemed a dangerous way to live.

I thought the same about a grayling butterfly I met with. The grayling is quite an individualist: it doesn't visit flowers very often and is also peculiar in its love of alighting on rocks or earth. Most of those we see in this district are on the slopes above the sea cliffs but we occasionally get them in our garden where, very rarely, we have seen one at the flowers of marjoram. But what butterfly, even a grayling, could totally resist the scent of marjoram? One August evening I saw what was for me an almost unique event—a butterfly choosing its bed for the night. Just before owl-light, and long after other butterflies had retired, I was strolling along the path to the estuary. In the dusk I saw a grayling (which I first mistook for a moth) flying back and forth along the track with a wild and rapid zigzag flight. In a few minutes it landed on a patch of bare ground and there it settled for the night. This seemed a hazardous place to sleep. Yet I daresay graylings have so roosted since the beginning of their time in the world.

On the shore I have on rare occasions seen a grayling visiting sea campion whose cushions of white flowers are such an adornment of coastal cliffs and shingle beaches. Here and there the campion has spread for miles up valleys near the sea, especially in the hinterland of Aberystwyth where it seems to have a curious affection for lead-mines. Unfortunately for this beautiful plant there is often a worm in the bud. Open a seed-pod and you may find little caterpillars eating the seeds. When I reared one of these caterpillars to find out what moth it would turn into, I had to wait till the following June for the answer: it was a lychnis moth. According to the books it could just as easily have been one of several related moths whose larvae all feed on campion seeds, moths such as the marbled coronet, the tawny shears and the campion moth. Sea campion is a versatile plant. Like thrift and scurvy-grass it also grows high on mountains. But up there I have not yet found its seeds being attacked by caterpillars though I suppose they must be at times.

★   ★   ★

It was with total astonishment in 1980 that I received an invitation to go and address the next annual meeting of the Thoreau Society of America in Concord, Massachusetts. It was, after all, getting on for thirty years since I had written my little life of Henry D. Thoreau (1817-62) when we were still living in our cottage in the valley of the

200

Einion; and I had long supposed the book was quite forgotten. Inevitably Concord was the one American town I had always wished to visit since it was there that Thoreau had lived and died, the writer-naturalist with whom I have always felt most at home. This is not only because of his passion for wilderness and because he was one of the first to speak up for its conservation. It is also because he saw that as we drift ever further from nature and simplicity in pursuit of a growth economy, the poorer must become the real quality of our lives.

On my first New England morning I was taken to Walden by bicycle while the day was still cool. I was led there by my hostess who, I was happy to find, was a Welsh lady who had settled in Concord but was still nostalgic about Radnorshire. So on July 10, 1981, I stood under the pines by the pond where my friend Thoreau, nearly 130 years earlier, had chosen to live for two years in near solitude in order to 'front the essential facts of life' and to gather the thoughts that were to tumble out later in that strange masterpiece: *Walden, or Life in the Woods*, first published in 1854.

Walden Pond, Concord, where Henry David Thoreau, aged 28, went to live and write for two years in a hut he built near the water's edge.

Henry D. Thoreau at the age of 37.
A crayon-drawing by A. L. Rowse.
Photograph by courtesy of the late
Leonard F. Kleinfeld of New York.

It was quite a moment for me to be actually there on Thoreau's patch of the earth, the still trees all round, the pond in complete tranquillity, its stony shallows sloping sharply into the depths a few yards offshore. A chipmunk fossicked for food at the site of Thoreau's cabin. Blue jays and grackles were noisy in the trees. A willow tit (which over there is a chickadee) called softly on a branch close to my ear, but if he was trying to give me a message from Thoreau I could not quite catch it.

As I stood there on that first morning I heard thunder in a clear blue sky, the thunder of a train going by high on its embankment near the far shore of the pond, just as Thoreau had seen the very first trains pass that way and which had helped to convince him he didn't like the way the nineteenth century was rushing towards industrialisation and ever more thoughtless exploitation of natural resources. A politicians' cliché of the time was that the people of America were progressing towards a 'manifest destiny' (an ancestor of today's American dream). Thoreau was unimpressed: 'The whole enterprise of this nation . . . is totally devoid of interest to me . . . No, they may go their way to their manifest destiny, which I trust is not mine'.

★   ★   ★

Before crossing the Atlantic I had speculated about what new birds I might meet with in Massachusetts. One I would be lucky to see, I was told, was a bluebird because, though abundant there in Thoreau's day, this popular symbol of happiness has now become scarce. So I was not surprised when I could find no bluebirds in Concord. But then I had the good fortune to be taken to Tyngsboro which is up near the border with New Hampshire and there I met Lillian Lund Files, a remarkable lady who for years has devoted her considerable energies to giving the bluebird a helping hand, not only by providing nest boxes on her twenty acres of grounds and elsewhere but also by promoting bluebird conservation in the press and by lecturing tirelessly in many states.

Lillian gave me the background story of bluebird conservation: how it was led by the North American Bluebird Society and supported by the Audubon Society and many local bird clubs. The bluebird's decline was due to multiple causes including loss of suitable living space caused by the spread of humanity and a lack of food because of the over-use of insecticides. Help for the bluebird consists mainly of the provision of huge numbers of nest boxes (over there they are often called 'bird houses') which are fastened to trees or posts and spaced out at intervals of about four to the mile in lines that stretch across country for hundreds of miles, reaching right up into Canada.

The boxes are needed because of the wholesale loss of holes in trees and fence-posts which used to be homes for bluebirds. What has happened is that many a dead or decaying tree, in these days of power-saws, has been cut down to provide fuel for wood-burning stoves; old hedgerows and orchards, always favourite bluebird habitats, have been cleared away; and the old-style wooden fence-posts, full of cavities in which to hide nests, have been replaced by metal posts.

Another problem is the competition for nest-holes from the ever-increasing population of house sparrows and starlings introduced long ago from Europe. To counter this menace many bluebird boxes are sited far from human habitations and therefore well away from sparrows; and their entrance holes are restricted to one and a half inches in diameter which makes them too small for starlings. There are also problems with native hole-nesters such as house wrens, tree swallows and others which are happy to nest in bluebird boxes. Would-be predators of bluebirds' nests are many, especially raccoons, red squirrels, domestic cats, and snakes; and bluebird conservationists are kept ever on their toes trying to outwit them. The happy result of all these efforts by so many willing hands is that there are now bluebirds breeding in many places where only a few years ago there were none.

The first time I ever heard of bluebirds was back in my college days when, as a student of French literature, I was an avid reader of the Belgian author, Maeterlinck, who wrote so well about nature. I was also charmed by his very popular play *The Bluebird* which tells of the adventures of two little children who go off to try (in vain of course) to capture the fairy-tale bluebird of happiness. It was not until I read Thoreau's *Walden* and began to know a little about American birds that I learned that there are in fact bluebirds in real life as well as in folklore and popular songs. Pink-breasted and blue-backed, they were inevitably called blue robins by the first British settlers who cherished them dearly and looked forward to their northward return every spring, just as we in Britain eagerly anticipate the first chiff-chaffs and swallows. And though not every modern New Englander has ever seen a bluebird, it is still a much loved bird.

In my two weeks in New England I saw other birds besides bluebirds that were very striking to my British eyes: cardinal, scarlet tanager, Baltimore oriole, cedar waxwing, wood duck, eastern kingbird, meadowlark and many more. I held a flicker (which is a woodpecker) in my hands and marvelled at its plumage details. And I was amazed to hear so much bird-song in the heat of mid-July, a month of near silence among most of the birds back home. Listening one evening to Concord's town band in the park, I heard with astonishment the beautiful song of a mocking bird which passionately accompanied the music from a nearby tree-top.

I was taken up the New Hampshire mountain called Monadnock, happy in the thought that Thoreau had been up there too. I was canoed far down Thoreau's river by a pale-face Minnehaha and saw turtles, killdeer plovers and spotted sandpipers as well as a wondrous show of the European purple loosestrife (*Lythrum salicaria*) which has colonised the river bank for miles, ousting the native flora. Botanists led me through the woods and showed me a bewildering new world of trees and wildflowers; but on some roadsides I felt completely at home where the native flora had long ago been replaced by aliens from Europe such as common St John's-wort, yellow toadflax, tufted vetch, yarrow, broad-leaved plantain and many others taken there by early settlers along with starlings and sparrows. When the native Indians saw all these alien plants creeping along the roadsides they called them 'white men's footprints'.

Concord was a memorable experience. I had seen something of the fauna and flora of a new continent. I had been given the warmest hospitality and made new friends. I had met eminent Thoreau scholars, among them Walter Harding who had generously helped me with my book nearly thirty years earlier; and Anne McGrath who, as that year's president of the Thoreau Society, had invited me to lecture. And when I got back home I re-read *Walden* with greater pleasure than ever. It says much for Thoreau's exactness of description that I had found his Walden world—the pond, the woods, the rivers —very much as I had always pictured them, except that one end of the pond had been grossly disfigured by a car-park and bathing facilities. Since then far worse clouds have gathered. Walden Woods are dangerously close to Boston and all that this implies in terms of the urbanisation of the countryside, and there have been recent threats of an office block and housing development. Against the vandals there are stalwart defenders fighting the good fight in defence of Thoreau's countryside. The creation of a Walden Pond National Park (the idea was first put forward by Thoreau himself in 1859) is now being campaigned for by conservationists under the banner *Walden Forever Wild*. To the great god, Pan, I pray for their success.

Towards the end of *Walden* we come to an unexpected throw-away line. Here is our author supposedly giving us an account of his two years by the pond. Yet when he has completed one year he suddenly closes the narrative saying: 'Thus was my first year's life in the woods completed; and the second year was similar to it'. That is all we ever hear about the second year!

So I will bring my story to a close by passing over the recent years of my life on the grounds that they have been similar to those which went before. Besides, now that we have caught up with Thoreau in his native Concord, what better subject to end with? I know he lived

205

a century and a half ago but he is truly a man of our time—a naturalist to his fingertips but concerned above all things with man's place in the environment. His writings were largely ignored in his lifetime and long afterwards. But today we are all in some way involved with, or are at least aware of, the plight of nature as pollution spreads, global warming threatens and habitats shrink while the human population expands out of control.

Today more than ever we need our Thoreaus to keep up our spirits. Thoreau himself would have nothing to do with pessimism. He was impressed by the cheerful courageousness of nature. Without it life on earth would have given up long ago in the face of all the disasters it has to cope with. 'The spruce, the hemlock and the pine will not countenance despair', he said in his essay, *Natural History in Massachusetts*. In his journal he wrote: 'If you are afflicted with melancholy... go to the swamp and see the brave spears of skunk-cabbage buds already advanced towards a new year... Do they seem to have lain down to die, despairing of skunk-cabbagedom?' Then at the end of *Walden*: 'The life in us is like the water in the river. It may rise this year higher than man has ever known it, and flood the parched uplands...'

Looking back to his birth in 1817 Thoreau reckoned it happened 'just in the nick of time'. He was right. His few decades were a wonderful period to be alive in Concord, then the centre of the flowering of New England thought and literature. There he was in the midst of it all and on intimate terms with Ralph Waldo Emerson and other luminaries. In fact it was while living under Emerson's roof that he wrote, or re-wrote, parts of *Walden*.

Born almost exactly a century after Thoreau, I too am thankful to have lived when I have. It is true that, far from experiencing anything like the flowering of New England, I have witnessed the de-flowering of Old England (and Wales) as the corncraky, herb-rich meadows have vanished one by one and so many lovely woodlands have gone. On the other hand I have seen the nature conservation movement grow from being a faint voice out in the wilderness to the considerable force it is today, involving not merely naturalists but a fair number of the general public who have been alerted as never before to nature's struggle for survival. I know it would have been better if conservation had taken root a century before it did. But we must be thankful that there is now a strong voice to speak out against public and private vandalism and all other threats to the natural environment. Mother Nature desperately needs every help she can get. Humanity too has an ever increasing need of nature reserves, for they are a contribution to our health and sanity. Thoreau's famous affirmation still stands: 'In wildness is the preservation of the world'.

Index

Aberdaron, 92
Aberdyfi, 53, 104, 183
Aberffraw, 124
Aberystwyth, 42, 50, 65, 74-5, 139, 200
  railway to Carmarthen, 82
Adder, 82-3
Aeron R., 131
Andorra, 160
Anglesey, 123-5
Ant, wood, 67, 126
Antennaria dioica, 86
Arddu, 34-5
Arnold, Richard, 194-5
Artists' Valley, 55
Atcham, 120-1

Backhouse, James, 141
Bala Lake, 126-7
Bardsey I., 10, 86-92
Barmouth, 8, 123
Bartlett, Eric, 188-9
Bartley Green, 6
Bats, 182
Bedstraw, northern, 155
Beeches in drought, 190
Beetle, oil, 67
Behrend, John and Mary, 119-20
Beinn Eighe, 167
Benoit, Peter, 101
Bentham, George, 95
Berwyn, 105-6
Best, Frank, 59-60, 84
Bettyhill, 167
Bevis, 11
Bewdley, 13, 33, 158
Bible, E.H.T., 53
Bilberry, 103
Bingley, William, 142
Bird Rock, 85-6

Birmingham, 1, 6, 20, 32
  University, 18
Blackbird, 13
Blackcock, 110
Bluebell, 179
Bluebird, 203-4
Borrow, George, 25, 194
Borth, 74, 182
  Bog, 72-4, 192
Bosherston, 30, 132
Botanical Gardens, 5
Botany, first steps in, 95
Boulder clay, 107
Bournville, 3, 31
Bowen, E. G., 125
Breconshire, 188-9
Breidden Hills, 121, 187, 188
Brimstone butterfly, 68
British Ecological Society, 84, 96
Brixham, 12
Brook, Arthur, 157
B.T.O. (British Trust for Ornithology), 14
Bunting, cirl, 31, 49
  snow, 68
Burren, 155-6
Bush-cricket, great green, 11
Buzzard, 12, 62-4, 171-2
Bwlch Einion, 115
Bwlch Gwair, 36-7, 39
Bwrdd Arthur, 124

Cader Idris, 10, 50, 96-8, 108
Cadman, Arthur, 59, 73, 106
Cae Dafydd, 33
Caer Caradoc, 1
Caerbwdi Bay, 133
Caernarfonshire, 86, 108
Caersws, 122
Camberwell beauty, 182-3

Harlech, 99
Harrier, hen, 177, 179
  Montagu's, 101, 150
Harthan, Anthony, 19-20
Hawkmoth, bedstraw, 159, 179
  convolvulus, 68
  eyed, 168
  hummingbird, 30
  lime, 1
  poplar, 1, 67
  privet, 30
  small elephant, 168
Hay Bluff, 188-9.
Heather, 39, 47, 103
Hengwm Annedd, 25, 29
Herefordshire, 13
Heron, 156, 157, 179
Hiawatha, Song of, 3, 4
Hibbert-Ware, Alice, 14
Hignett, Mary, 140, 188
Hillyfields, 2
Holt Fleet, 158
Holyhead Mountain, 124
Hoopoe, 123
Hore, 25
Housman, A. E., 1, 32-3, 120
Hunter, N. C., 169
Huxley, Sir Julian, 38-9

Inchnadamph, 167
Inglis-Jones, Elizabeth, 78, 80
Ingram, Geoffrey, 156, 157
Ireland, 155-6

Jefferies, Richard, 11, 31
Jenkins, Tom, 115
Jermy, Clive, 151
Jersey, 48-9
Johnes, Thomas, 43, 78, 80
Johnson, Thomas, 141
Jones, D. A., 141
  Elizabeth, 21
  E. W., 126
  Gwyneth, 140

Juniper, 108, 166, 197

Kenfig, 157
Kestrel, 69
Kingfisher, 177
Kite, black-winged, 153
  Committee, 47
  red, 43-7, 157
  talon-locking, 185-6
Kittiwake, 76, 136-7
Koch, Ludwig, 38

Ladybird invasion, 191
Lambourne, Cecil and Jonny, 87, 155, 165, 175
Lead-mines, 21-2, 106
Leasowes, 4
Leighton redwoods, 121
Lenton, Libby, 180
Leopard, 162
Lhuyd, Edward, 85-6, 106, 141, 150, 151, 160, 187
Lion, 162-3
Lizard, 196
Llanbedr, 123
Llandogo, 125-6
Llandudno, 113-14
Llandysiliogogo, 76
Llangollen, 155
Llangorse Lake, 189
Llanymynech Hill, 140
Llanrhaeadr, 105
Llanuwchllyn, 160
Lloyd, Bertram, 83
Lloyd-George's grave, 33
Llyn Cwm Bychan, 102
  Morwynion, 102
  Tegid, 126-7
Loch Maree, 167
Lochdyn, 77
Lockley, Ronald, 35-6, 37, 48, 80, 86, 94
London N.H.S., 176
Long Mountain, 120-1

212

Wheatear, 28, 39
Whimbrel, 49
Whinchat, 40
White, Gilbert, 93-4
Whitethroat, 16
Whitlowgrass, yellow, 108
Wigeon, 138
Williams, Ken, 179
  Peter, 142
Williams-Ellis, Rupert and Cecily,
  86-7
Williamson, Henry, 31
Winter moth, 198-9
Winters, severe, 37-8, 138, 143-4
Woodgate, 3
Woodlark, 49, 52, 120, 144
Woodpecker, black, 146-7
  great spotted, 181-2
Woodsia, oblong, 108, 150-1
Woofferton, 33
Worcester, 158

Worcestershire, 13, 18, 19
Wright, Harold, 12, 13, 21, 32-3,
  39, 42-7, 65, 66
Wroxeter, 120
Wye R., 23, 24, 125
Wyre Forest, 19, 33

Yellow underwing, 182
Yellow-legs, lesser, 175
Ynys Dewi, *see* Ramsey
  Edwin, 115, 119, 139, 145, 161,
  174
  Enlli, *see* Bardsey
  Gwylan, 92-3
Ynys-hir, 65, 115, 169-70, 176
Ynys-las, 71-2
Youth Hostels, 21
Yr Arddu, 34-5
Ystwyth R., 106

Zambia, 20, 151